Breaking the Barrier

Margaret A. Judson

BREAKING THE BARRIER

A PROFESSIONAL AUTOBIOGRAPHY
BY A WOMAN EDUCATOR AND HISTORIAN
BEFORE THE WOMEN'S MOVEMENT

Rutgers
The State University of New Jersey
New Brunswick, New Jersey

Library of Congress Cataloging in Publication Data

Judson, Margaret Atwood, 1899–
    Breaking the barrier.

    1. Judson, Margaret Atwood, 1899–   . 2.
Douglass College—Faculty—Biography. 3. Educa-
tors—United States—Biography. 4. Historians—
United States—Biography. 5. College teachers—
United States—Biography. I. Title.

LD4759.5.D68J83   1984   370'.92'4   [B]   84–11690
                ISBN 0–88111–004–3

To my students
1929–1967

Contents

CONTENTS

Illustrations

Preface

THIS PROFESSIONAL AUTOBIOGRAPHY is essentially written from memory, for I never kept a diary. For bibliographical facts I am indebted to the Rutgers Alexander Library and for old college catalogs to the Douglass Library. During the first year of my work, a faculty study allotted to me by the Alexander Library proved to be most helpful. And much as I believe in the recognition of women I still prefer to use the term "man" in the generic sense rather than to use the word "person."

The first draft of my manuscript was read by Professors Jessie Lutz and Mary Hartman, who made numerous valuable suggestions and urged me to continue the work. Later my friends Ruth Adams, Elizabeth Ellis, Carol Hageman, Helen Martin, Herbert Rowen, and Virginia Whitney read it. Each of them made helpful comments, for which I sincerely thank them. The acute memory of Elizabeth Kimball concerning the people and events at the early meetings of the Berkshire conference of women historians was a great help. I am also indebted to the editor, Martyn Hitchcock, for his careful work.

It is impossible to thank adequately Ruth Adams, a former Douglass dean, Henry Winkler, a long-time colleague who became the Rutgers vice president, and Mary Hartman, the present Douglass dean, for their three generous tributes to me. I sincerely appreciate the generosity of the many friends and historians from California to England who subscribed to the autobiography before its publication.

It was the support of the Rutgers administration and the untiring efforts of Mary Hartman which made possible the publication of this work.

Margaret A. Judson
April 2, 1984

Appreciations

Appreciations

WHEN MARGARET JUDSON is delighted, her eyes shine and sparkle. Take Margaret at the bridge table. When her bid produces her partner's dummy, all is serious. Her face is sober, her choices deliberate, her risks calculated. But when the last card falls and the bid is made, her head comes up triumphantly and her eyes are bright, merry and brilliant, illuminating a happy face.

When Margaret Judson is irritated, she splutters. Take the case of the psychology department's rats. There was a time where, for lack of other space, these rodents were housed in the basement, directly under Margaret's office. Not ingratiating neighbors at any time, in warm weather they made themselves loathsome. At such times, the Dean could expect a visit from Margaret, to put the case that something *had* to be done. And, unlike her usual delivery, the tirade came in fragments, explosions, short bursts of almost inexpressible fury. It cannot be said that the outbursts occasioned the provision of the Pysch building, but they may have accelerated its construction.

When Margaret Judson is deeply angry, it is always for good cause. Her wrath is righteous. And she expresses it deliberately, quietly, logically, judiciously. Reason's coolness, passion's heat produce a tension that is even physical, in the quiet tautness of body, in the measured speech. Margaret angry is to be reckoned with.

Margaret Judson has great courage, if you share my belief that courage is the prerequisite for the exercise of virtue.

Her honesty permeates all her activities. As a scholar, she neglects the obvious and superficial in favor of the truth beneath. She has known the researcher's "tragedy," the destruction of a lovely theory in the face of an inescapable fact, and has abandoned the attractive for the actual. This holds in personal and professional relations, too. We remember the faculty meetings when she spoke directly, openly, requiring always that her colleagues recognize all elements in the matter under discussion. One does not suppress or pervert evidence. And she was as direct, though kindly, in dealing with individuals. When as department chairman she had to present unpleasant truths to a colleague, she did it clearly. One knew where one stood with Margaret.

Margaret Judson has a capacity for hard work. Her industry meant that her teaching was never stinted, in the busiest of times. Legions of students, undergraduate and graduate, assemble to testify to the careful preparation of her lectures, the unobtrusive guidance of her discussion sessions, the meticulousness of her readings of their papers. At the same time, she was serving on the committees—college, university, professional—that needed her participation. And always, though not easily or as freely as she would have wished, her own research made its claims, which she strove to meet.

Margaret Judson is generous, with all that she commands. To her colleagues in the history department she was always available for good advice and encouragement. She was the first to praise their accomplishments and rejoice in public recognition thereof. And her good feelings did not stop at the boundaries of her own discipline; faculty members in all departments, as they deserved it, won Margaret's tribute. Her fellow historians in the wider plain of scholarship gained her outspoken admiration and praise for their work, as *they* deserved it; there is no professional jealousy in Margaret but rather delight in good work, whoever does it. She has been especially concerned for and active in the interest of young women historians, training and encouraging them to be effective professionals, fostering their careers realistically and thoughtfully, and delighting in their progress and accomplishments. She has her own "network," and an affectionate and appreciative one it is. She has been generous even to deans! What I owe her, what Polly Bunting, Margery Foster, Jewel Cobb and Mary Hartman owe her cannot be repaid. And what a good dean she herself was!

Margaret Judson has a capacity for loyalty, to institutions, to people. As she recalls her years of study, her devotion to Mt. Holyoke illuminates her account of classes, games, wild mischief, and happy fellowship. Radcliffe and Harvard, with their resources for the scholar, have her respect and honor. But her own institutions are Douglass and Rutgers, whose well-being has never fallen out of her concern. Her often expressed conviction that they can be the best of institutions has made her an enthusiastic advocate—and an equally enthusiastic critic, when criticism was needed. She chastens only those about whom she deeply cares. The Berkshire Conference, the Conference on British Studies, received in their early years her tenacious attention and in their maturity her unwavering support. And while Margaret continues to extend her circle of friends, young and old, she can happily catalog a list of "avid acquaintance." Her loyalty to friends of long standing delights them and—we hope—pleases her.

This catalog of her virtues returns again and again to her relations with people. Margaret Judson is a true humanist in that people are important to her. And her own humanity, her self-respect and self-confidence, shows in most ingratiating ways. For example, Margaret has standards for her personal appearance. Not for her any academic casualness or untidiness; the crisp suits, the perky print dresses, give her as much pleasure as they do us. Life is to be enjoyed—late on a sunny afternoon, for instance, on the deck hanging out over the lake at Spofford, with a pleasing drink at hand, dinner under control in the little kitchen, and several fortunate guests discussing seriously or laughing happily with her.

People are in her debt, and I speak for so many of us in once again saying "Thank you."

Ruth M. Adams
Dartmouth College

I FIRST MET Margaret Judson at the home of Elizabeth and Ethan Ellis sometime in late 1947. One of a group of young assistant professors recruited unsystematically but effectively by Irving S. Kull, I was fresh out of the Navy and my last year at graduate school, woefully ignorant of the real world of academia. The Ellises, I came to realize, recognized our insecurity and, in an understated way that suggested rural New England rather than their middle-western roots, acted as mentors for the un-initiated. I knew vaguely that the New Jersey College for Women was associated with Rutgers, but Margaret Judson was the first colleague from across town whom I met in my first year of service in New Brunswick.

My reaction that first evening was quite neutral. I knew even less about Miss Judson than I did about N.J.C. *The Crisis of the Constitution*, which was to make her scholarly reputation, had not yet been published. All I had been told was that she taught both history and political theory at the women's college. Before the Second World War, I had worked close-ly at the University of Chicago with Frances Gillespie, the author of a major study of British trade union politics in the nineteenth century, and I could guess at how tough-minded and thick-skinned any academic woman had to be to succeed in the professorial male world of the twenties and thirties. But certainly Margaret Judson, however tough-minded she might be, did not resemble the picture, un-doubtedly a caricature, that I had in my mind. She was pleasant, cultivated, interested apparently in learning about my interests as well as talking about her own (not a universal trait among academicians), and, if it is permitted to use the term these days, very much a lady.

She was all that, but how much more! As I grew to know her better, I became aware that here was one of the linch-pins of the institution, a distinguished scholar whose work brought luster to our department, a demanding teacher whose students regarded her with affectionate awe, a thoughtful and considerate colleague whose first concerns were for the welfare and the integrity of her college and her university. Her *Crisis of the Constitution* was not published until 1949, but by the early fifties it was apparent that she had made not simply an important, but one of the four or five major interpretative explorations of seventeenth-century England. Her constitutional analysis quickly became an essential backdrop for the understanding of the complicated political and economic issues that had captivated the attention of so many other scholars.

Yet in the early fifties, although a neophyte historian like myself had his own graduate seminar and supervised advanced graduate work, Miss Judson had no opportunity to participate in the advanced graduate instruction directed by the Rutgers College department. Dean Margaret Corwin of N.J.C., perhaps rightly although it appeared parochial to some of us young Turks, felt that she could not afford to lose the teaching time, since there was no mechanism for "crediting" the college for the graduate participation of its faculty. I must say that some of my senior colleagues at Rutgers College were less than enthusiastic about sharing prerogatives with a woman from N.J.C. It took several years of negotiation, but eventually we worked out a deal. I crossed town to N.J.C. and taught a section of introductory history while Margaret came over to "Rutgers" to offer a seminar in seventeenth-century England. As a result, I gradually came to know many more of my N.J.C. colleagues than did most faculty members at the men's colleges. Above all, I made a valued new friend in Miss Judson.

Over the years we talked of many things besides English history: political discussions during the McCarthy era, when her strong instinct for social order clashed with her deep concern for individual rights; learned assessments of the comparative skills of the Boston Red Sox (she was misguided enough to be a Boston fan) and the Cincinnati Reds during the great World Series of 1975; shrewd and almost always generous perceptions of the foibles of various colleagues. I often drove Margaret and our mutual friend Elizabeth Kimball to meetings of the Conference on British Studies which she helped found. There it was impossible not to observe the regard and the interest with which the Jack Hexters or the Lawrence Stones or other of the giants in her field regard the author of *The Crisis of the Constitution*.

The same was true of N.J.C., or Douglass College

as it became in 1955. For some years I taught an interdisciplinary course with Ruth Adams, dean of Douglass College, whose talents I admired and whose friendship I cherished. Again and again, Ruth talked about consulting Margaret on some tangled issue of college policy. Whether it was a matter of academic standards or faculty politics or a wide range of student concerns, she could always look to her for cool judgment, solid common sense, and often real wisdom. When Miss Adams left to become president of Wellesley College, she told me how delighted she was that Margaret Judson had agreed to be acting dean until a successor could be chosen.

Like so many other colleagues, Margaret Judson was kind and helpful to my first wife during the last painful years of her life. When I remarried, my new spouse and she seemed to hit it off famously. Both became members at about the same time of a literary group, The Travellers, of which Margaret writes in her memoir. Bea would report again and again how the professor, of whom most of the women were in awe, put everyone at ease while at the same time encouraging them to higher standards of performance by her own lucid and exemplary papers. I must say I was fascinated to observe the empathy between the somewhat reserved daughter of a Congregational minister and the rather more uninhibited offspring of a Jewish garment worker. But then, I thought, my mother, like Margaret, had been born in Winsted, Connecticut. Perhaps that, in some wildly illogical way, explained the affinity. However that may be, Margaret was one of a small group of women—Jane Burks, Suzanne Schlatter, Mary Liz Bredemeier in particular—who served as mentors to a neophyte academic spouse, just as she served as mentor to first-rate younger academic professionals like Mary Hartman or Alison Olson.

The tone and the flavor of any university is set by a small number of people—a handful of exceptional scholars, a few outstanding teachers, even an occasional gifted administrator. For Rutgers, Margaret Judson is surely among that small number. But for so many of us who served the university with her, much as we have valued her as a scholar, a teacher, an administrator, we have been many more times enriched simply because she is our friend.

Henry R. Winkler
The University of Cincinnati

MARGARET JUDSON had already retired from her teaching and administrative duties at Douglass College of Rutgers when I had the good fortune to meet her in the late nineteen-sixties. She was then doing research on a new book; but she took time to get to know me, just as she took time to get to know other new members of the history department. Her interest was genuine, and I was flattered. (Margaret more than made up for the colleague who habitually called me by the name of the only other young woman in the department.) Soon she introduced me to many of her friends among the faculty and administrators at the university. I was a new instructor still working on my dissertation, but Margaret Judson gave me the heady feeling of being a protégée. That she took me seriously helped persuade me that I could take myself seriously. This, I have learned since, has been her gift to many a fortunate young scholar. And it is all the more precious for being unselfconsciously given.

Not long after I defended my Ph.D., Margaret invited me, with some ceremony, to attend the annual meeting of the Berkshire Conference of Women Historians. The group had been founded in the twenties by some women who were irritated by their exclusion from conferences that male colleagues were then holding at Lake Placid; and Margaret, who attended the second meeting and was later to preside over the group, came to hold the most faithful attendance record. She also probably has the distinction of introducing the largest number of new members. I confess that I was wary when I learned that the annual spring meetings of the Berkshire Conference included only one or two formal presentations and a business meeting, that the rest of the time was spent hiking, visiting local sites, or just sitting around talking in the picturesque New England inns where the conferences were held. To an uptight, would-be professional too sensitive to male colleagues' jibes about "going off to pick flowers," it all sounded vaguely frivolous. How wrong I was!

The Berkshire Conference, as Margaret well knew, was and is a superb support network for women historians (though she would never use such jargon in describing it). It is a first-class collection of women whose ties now span the generations from graduate student to retiree. And when, back in 1972, the Berks trusted Lois Banner and me in our idea to have the group sponsor a whole conference on the new field of women's history, it was Margaret Judson who managed to convince a number of skeptical members that the notion was not wholly without merit. Soon she became one of the most enthusiastic boosters of the new history of women. The first conference, held at Douglass College, would be followed by conferences at Radcliffe, Bryn Mawr, Mount Holyoke, Vassar, and—in 1984 —at Smith. Margaret has attended most of them.

Still, the annual meetings of the "little Berks" remain the heart of the organization. And throughout the seventies on a spring weekend, the Douglass-Rutgers contingent would head off together toward the Berkshires with Margaret, who knew the countryside better than all of us, serving as navigator and tourguide. Conversations ranged from current events (Margaret always seemed to have the day's *New York Times* committed to memory), to research projects and problems, hassles in the history department, and the occasional trials of being a woman in academe. Margaret always resisted our efforts to get her to join in these latter discussions of indignities, lovingly recounted in the new tongue of our feminist anger. Later we would learn what we had suspected: that Margaret had some tales to top our own. She mentions a few in these pages, but it is not her style to relish in the telling. Once, as we motored our way through rural Massachusetts and conversations lingered on these themes, Margaret's impatience became palpable. "Girls!" she exclaimed. "You're missing this beautiful scenery!" And so we were.

In May 1978, when the Berks celebrated their fiftieth anniversary, it was my pleasure as the new president to organize a panel of members from different generations, with Margaret Judson as "senior stateswoman." All the participants talked about what the Berks had meant to their lives, and the evening was emotional and unforgettable. Leading off, a hardly aloof but still formidable personage to the younger members, Margaret reminded us that she, too, had once been a somewhat uncertain new-comer to the Berks. She charmed us with confessions that she had been rather awed by the austere elders, such as Elizabeth Hodder and Judith Blow Williams from Wellesley, who disdained to join the hiking parties and sat the weekend long on the wicker rocking chairs of the Victorian porches. But returning each spring, Margaret explained how she had come to feel part of an extended family whose older, more experienced members helped the younger ones along.

And Margaret Judson had had more than a fair share of obstacles for a young scholar, including frail health, heavy family responsibilities, and de-manding teaching loads. Through it all, she kept at her scholarship and produced, in *The Crisis of the Constitution*, a work which remains in print and stands as a classic in the field. Margaret never dwells on the difficulties she encountered along the way, however; and though she has a justified sense of pride in achievement, she is a good deal more modest than most of us would be tempted to be in her place. I recall, too, that she explained to the Berks members on that anniversary evening that the uncomplaining attitude which so mystified some of the more youthful members was no special vir-tue. In those days of the depression, she stated, you just did not complain if you had a job.

How happy I and all of us at the University are that that job was with *us*, at the New Jersey College for Women—now Douglass College—of Rutgers! From 1928 until 1966, young women had the gift of her rigorous yet compassionate instruction. And members of the faculty and staff, too, appreciated her wisdom, her sense of humor, and her deep commitment to women's education. In celebrating her, the colleagues and former students inscribed in this volume of her memoirs represent the legions of those whose lives she touched as teacher, scholar, administrator, and cherished friend. My own debt to Margaret cannot be repaid. But like all those here, I can pay tribute to a dear friend and a personal heroine.

Mary S. Hartman
Douglass College

Breaking
the Barrier

Introduction

WHY IN THE WORLD, a reader may well ask, should you, a retired professor, 84 years old, write your professional autobiography as a woman professor, historian, and educator in the years before the women's movement? Only since my retirement in 1967 have I become interested in women's history and in particular in that of college and university professors. What was your own experience? my younger academic women and men friends ask. Were there not many doors barred against you? Did you not find that financial rewards were unfairly distributed, and at times was there not insulting treatment of you because of your sex? Please write that sad story down while you are alive. We need it, so some ardent feminist historians often said, as one more small segment in women's history.

This story, however, will surprise some of those urging me to write it. Of course it will include frustrations and inequities, but only in part. For it tells of many opportunities and satisfactions, and, I believe, some successes along the way.

3

Family and Community
Background

THINKING BACK on the early years in Winsted, the town in northwestern Connecticut where I was born and where I lived for eighteen years, I now realize how much I owe to my family and to that community. Not that I ever thought or expressed a desire to be a college professor. How I loved being with the gang—my girlfriends and boyfriends—skating, yes even skiing in 1910, sliding down steep, dangerous hills on double rippers, playing baseball with hard balls, and loving tennis too! We girls organized a secret club, which met in dark corners of Madeline's attic. On an afternoon, both girls and boys would gather around the Gaylords' piano, while Dolly played and we sang popular songs—"I've Been Working on the Railroad All the Live Long Day," "Swing Low Sweet Chariot," and one whose title I've forgotten but which included these delightful lines: "I've got rings on my

4

fingers and bells on my toes, elephants to ride upon," etc.

These activities were great fun, but so also was reading (fortunately there was no television to watch for hours on end.) Books contained fascinating stories and widened one's curiosity and interest in the world around us. Most important of all in my pre-adolescent education was my father, a Congregational minister and a graduate of Yale and Yale Divinity School. He patiently answered my many questions and encouraged and guided me, though a mere girl, in my curiosity and widening interests. On a small ministerial salary, he bought an encyclopedia of several volumes for younger people and urged me to find answers to many of my questions. How I appreciate the fact that he encouraged me to make up my own mind when faced with a difficult problem!

In one of the ten rooms of the large parsonage hung a large map of the United States which was fascinating to explore. Years later, when teaching freshman history at Douglass, I often asked the janitor to bring the heavy set of historical maps to the room where my class was held. One of my colleagues told me that the janitor had remarked to him that "Miss Judson must have been born with a map in her mouth."

Although my father held liberal views, my Sunday-school teacher felt drinking any alcohol at all was sinful. In 1912, before prohibition, she asked the dozen or so girls in her class to promise that they would never drink alcohol. The only one refusing to promise was the minister's daughter, who said that, although she never had tasted an alcoholic beverage, she might want to sometime in the future. Obviously shocked, the good lady complained of my refusal to my father, who calmly replied that his daughter had made up her own mind on that issue.

While my father encouraged my intellectual curiosity, my mother cared for her sickly child, who in her first seven years had not only the usual childhood diseases, but a severe, prolonged bout with whooping cough, which kept her out of school for a year. She also contracted malarial fever, which subsequently returned each spring for several years in milder form. On a slim budget, mother, an excellent cook, produced well-balanced nourishing meals. In the days before hamburger, she squeezed beef through her old-fashioned meat grinder, to give extra strength to her anaemic child. It was she who encouraged my love of the outdoors and of sports, believing it a good counterbalance to my love of books. Since she was a fine musician with a lovely soprano voice, it was a terrible disappointment to her that I had no musical ability. In later years, however, I came to love music, attending many concerts, and listening to classical music on my stereo. When friends of my parents called in the evening, there was interesting conversation. My father had been to Palestine in 1898 and both father and mother to western Europe in 1910.[1] Mrs. Fred Strong, a Wellesley graduate, was my favorite caller, perhaps because she brought into the discussion ideas and points of view unknown to me. Quietly listening to the conversation of the elders, I hoped that my presence and bedtime hour would be forgotten.

As an only child was I spoiled? I doubt it, but who am I to say? Two doors away the Gaylord family lived with five children, the youngest of whom, Dolly, was my best friend. Mr. Gaylord, a tall, handsome man, teased me as he did Dolly; and Mrs. Gaylord always made this single child welcome in her home, where I spent many hours. In later years, when she was over ninety and a frail invalid, I visited her in Winsted, and gave her a copy of my *Crisis of the Constitution*. She seemed as happy to see me and receive it as if it had been written by one of her own children.

Although Winsted was an industrial town, situ-

1. Father's way was paid, as he conducted the tour for a small group of friends, who had asked him to do so.

7

ated on the Mad and Still rivers, it was a community far enough away from the nearest big city, Hartford, to have many cultural activities. To the town's Opera House came an occasional New York play. How I loved the play *Little Women*, even though I wept buckets of tears when Jo refused to marry Laurie! Renowned lecturers from New York or Boston would speak in the winter to large audiences in one of the churches. Above all, there was the Choral Union, where each week in the winter over a hundred men and women met and learned to sing a cantata—"Elijah," for example, under the baton of a conductor from New York. In June the Winsted chorus joined the well-trained choruses of Torrington, Norfolk, and Canaan. Here for three nights in early June a musical festival was held on the beautiful grounds of the Stoeckels', who were its sponsors and financial backers.[2] An orchestra made up of players from the Philharmonic and the Metropolitan Opera accompanied the joint chorus, while the soloists I remember were Louise Homer and Geraldine Farrar. On the third night, the orchestra performed—again with renowned guests—and one year Kreisler and Zimbalist played a duet. In June

2. No tickets could be bought for the concerts. Members of the chorus were given them, and since both mother and father sang in the chorus, they had many tickets to give to relatives and friends.

1914 I was allowed to attend and privileged to hear Jan Sibelius give his first and (I believe) only appearance in this country.[3] After he led the orchestra in the *Finlandia*, the audience spontaneously rose to its feet, stamping and shouting its approval. Two or three years ago a speaker on the radio commented that all the music lovers of America were present to hear Sibelius on that visit. Perhaps I, who was fourteen, remain one of the few in that audience still alive.

3. His intended tour of America was cancelled because of the outbreak of World War One.

Grammar School

I REMEMBER VERY LITTLE about the first few
grades in grammar school. In the Fifth grade,
however, Miss Woodward, an excellent teacher,
introduced me to new and fascinating areas of ge-
ography. By the time we graduated from the Eighth
grade, most of the class could write grammatically
and handle arithmetical problems, including frac-
tions and decimals. I particularly remember the
Eighth-grade teacher who demonstrated the intricacies of working out square roots.

As for history, I learned more from my father
and my own reading than from any teacher. A
child's book on Queen Victoria and her family given
me by my uncle's English wife must have started my
interest in England and its royal family, for I can
still name all of Victoria's nine children. To recite
the names of England's kings—William the Con-
queror, William his son, then Henry, Stephen, and
Henry, Richard, and John became a favorite ditty.
King Arthur and his knights came alive when our
group engaged in their knightly combats. My father

carved and painted for Sir Launcelot (me) a beautiful wooden sword to flash around in our play.

Somehow American history seemed less interesting than British, although I read in the encyclopedia given me all the military details of the Battle of Gettysburg unconcerned, I'm afraid, over the terrible slaughter and loss of human life. "Barbara Fritchie" and "Sheridan's Ride to Winchester Forty Miles away" were among my favorite poems. When World War One broke out, I remember the exact spot on Walnut Street where a friend said she was for the Germans while I proclaimed that I was for the English. Father, also supporting the English, abandoned his longtime ministerial refusal to buy a Sunday newspaper, and now bought one, but only after church.

As valedictorian from grammar school, I wrote and read at commencement my first historical paper. And on what topic? The seventeenth-century regicides who fled to America after the Restoration of Charles II and hid in such places as New Haven, Connecticut, and Hadley, Massachusetts. The choice of this subject was mine, for I had heard and read about the New England hideouts of the English regicides. "Research" for the English background and the American side of the story was pursued in two books, available in the Winsted library. The audience at graduation seemed to like the paper, but my pleasure was dampened when the mother of a good friend of mine, who had no part in the program, remarked that "of course her father wrote it." Neither my father nor my mother had read or heard any of it before I formally delivered it at commencement. Was it an augury for the fact that years later seventeenth-century England became my major area of research and writing?

On reading again my first historical essay, which was "no masterpiece," I can at least state that it was grammatically correct and quite interesting.

High School

THE WINSTEAD HIGH SCHOOL was the Gilbert
School, well endowed by the Gilbert Clock
Company in the town and open free of charge
to Winsted children, whereas residents of nearby
Norfolk and New Hartford had to pay a small sum
to attend. In 1980 I was shocked when I read in
the *New York Times* an obituary on the death of
Michael Halberstan. He had been brought up, according to the obituary, in Winsted, a "mill town
in northwestern Connecticut," but had attended a
fine high school in New York City—implying, of
course, that the Winsted high school must have
been pretty poor.

It certainly was not. My courses there consisted
of four years of Latin, three of French, two of German (still taught during the war years 1914–1918),
four of English, three of mathematics, two of history, one of home economics. Greek and chemistry
were also available, and in later years I was sorry I
didn't take them. For those not planning to go to

college, a secretarial business course for girls and a manual training one for boys were offered.

I'm afraid that the two courses in ancient history failed to stimulate my interest in the subject, for the teacher was primarily an English teacher. It was believed at that time (and I'm afraid it still is at times today) that anyone who could read needed no special knowledge, training, or skill to teach history. This high-school teacher expected her class to recite verbatim what the text book had stated, with no class discussion, controversy, or additions to the text. I still remember that on a quiz in ancient history Miss Dibble asked, "What in your opinion" was the most important battle in the Persian wars? Aware that the text said Marathon, I said Thermopylae, arguing that all the Greek forces were engaged there, whereas only the Athenians were at Marathon. On that quiz I received a C, instead of the usual A, and, though I thought it unfair, kept quiet (perhaps because I was a girl). Then a red-headed young Irishman, Timothy Bannon, who had given a similar answer, challenged the teacher. Courageously I came to his support, but our efforts failed to change her attitude or our low marks. I wonder if Miss Dibble ever knew that later Timothy received Phi Beta Kappa at Yale, and I at Mt. Holyoke. In 1968 at our fiftieth high-school class reunion, Timothy greeted me enthusiastically, asking if I remembered our battle against Miss Dibble. I did.

Despite poor teaching in history, I still must have cared for the subject. In the spring of 1918 for the senior paper in English I chose Poland—its partition in the eighteenth century, its attempts in the nineteenth to become independent, and its aspirations and opportunities, at the time I was writing, to achieve its independence after Germany was defeated.

Mathematics and English were the subjects I loved in high school, for in each the teacher was excellent. In algebra and geometry Miss Stafford skillfully demonstrated difficult and intricate problems on the blackboard, pausing at intervals to solicit a student's help in their solution. In freshman English Miss Bates wisely chose (I believe) to begin the course with the stories of classical mythology, hoping thereby to lay a solid foundation for the many references to them in later literature. The books read (Scott's *Talisman*, for example) led to lively class discussions, and our written work was carefully corrected. Would that Misses Stafford and Bates were alive now, so that I might thank them for opening so many doors for inquiring adolescent minds.

Whether or not the Gilbert School class of 1918 was exceptional, I don't know. When, however, I recently discovered and looked over the large high-school picture of the class, I was amazed by the number, almost a third, who went on to college. Out of a class of about fifty, eight or nine boys went on to college—three or four to Yale, one to Johns Hopkins, and the others to places I cannot recall. For boys to go to college then was not unusual, but from our class eight girls also went—four to Mt. Holyoke, two to Smith, one to the Pratt Institute, and I'm not sure where the eighth girl went. At that time, students in the upper echelons of their class could enter these colleges without examinations, but I remember tutoring Dolly for her entrance examinations to Smith, where she was accepted and from which she graduated in 1922. It speaks well for the excellent training given us at Gilbert that, out of the sixteen going to college from the class of 1918, four received Phi Beta Kappa, two at Yale and two at Mt. Holyoke.

Although our high-school years coincided with World War One, we were not too interested or concerned about such far-away events. Instead, there was the next high-school dance held on Friday or Saturday night. After an exciting basketball game, also taking place on the weekend, our beaux took us to the new Palace of Sweets where we feasted on its concoctions—banana splits being the newest and most delicious. This Palace was run by the Armenian or Lebanese father of Ralph Nader, who later graduated from Gilbert School, as did his sister, today a professor of anthropology at Stanford. Perhaps the most exciting event of the winter was a sleigh-ride in a large truck on runners, driven by sturdy horses on the snowy roads. Here your date helped keep you warm, sometimes kissed you, but made no further advances; certainly there were no drinks or drugs.

In retrospect I realize how fortunate it was that I was born and reared in Winsted, this industrial town at the head of the Naugutuck valley with its outstanding high school and its community life and culture. Today, when many historians are turning to local history to deepen our understanding of the past, I suggest that a study of Winsted would be an excellent topic for some historian to undertake.

Mount Holyoke

Aᴺᴰ ɴᴏᴡ ᴄᴏʟʟᴇɢᴇ—to which I almost didn't go, because of my father's health problems and financial reverses. Nevertheless, he insisted I must go, taking some of his meager savings to make it possible. At that time there were no federal grants or loans and too few college scholarships. After my freshman year I received a small annual scholarship, but for two years I waited on table (badly), and then, as a senior, lived in a cheaper, fourth-floor room and tutored several freshmen in mathematics.[1] My new college wardrobe consisted of two gingham dresses, a pleated wool skirt, and the inevitable beloved middy blouses.

Why did I choose Mt. Holyoke? Friends invited me to visit it, along with Wellesley, and Smith. In 1918 the fees for all were approximately the same, about $500 per year. Smith was not my choice because of its location in the midst of a small city, whereas a country setting appealed to me. The beau-

1. Roberta Teale Swartz '25, later the college poet, was one freshman I tutored in mathematics.

tiful extensive Wellesley campus delighted me. Furthermore, it was my mother's choice because of her admiration for her friend, Mrs. Fred Strong, a Wellesley graduate. However, on the Saturday when I was visiting there, all the students seemed to have left campus and taken off to Boston, many to its theaters. Well aware that on an allowance of $5 per *month* such a weekend spree was impossible, I decided that Wellesley was not for me. Did I, a future historian, opt for Mt. Holyoke because of its outstanding history department? Not at all— the fact is simply that on the Saturday afternoon I spent there, the campus was alive with girls playing tennis, baseball or hockey, or just strolling around.

Girls living in co-ed dormitories today can hardly imagine the strict rules controlling our conduct in those far-off years. On a beautiful autumn afternoon in 1918, several boys from Winsted appeared and invited their friends in South Hadley to ride with them to Amherst. There we picked apples, returning to our dormitories before dinner. Next morning, however, came the decree that we would be campused for two months, because we should have asked permission to leave the campus and drive with boys—even in the afternoon.

In the winter of my sophomore year I deliberately broke the rule that on Sunday students might not ski, although after church they were allowed to snowshoe. On snowshoes, so the rule was explained, students quietly walked through the woods, whereas on the hills where they skied they broke the Sabbath calm by shouting to each other when they fell down or had a successful trip down the slopes. One Sunday afternoon Professor Neilson, a near neighbor of those living in Sycamores, our small dormitory, dropped by on her skis to see if any of the girls would join her in a walk through the snowy woods. Delighted to accept her invitation, I secured my skis (no other girl possessed a pair), and off we went for a *quiet* winter stroll through the woods.

Much as I enjoyed my freshman year, the required course of study could have been more challenging—at least for a good student from a superior high school. To require a fifth year of Latin seemed ridiculous, but we never thought of questioning the authority or wisdom of the faculty in insisting upon it. Nor did we suggest that Latin was "irrelevant" for our times. Knowing my fondness for history, a friend and recent graduate had advised me to ask for Professor Putnam in this subject, but I was assigned to a one-year replacement professor. Somehow screwing up my courage to approach the formidable registrar, Miss Carolyn Green, I asked if I might be transferred to Miss Putnam's class. Speaking with authoritative finality, Miss Green replied: "Of course not." In English, however, my teacher was Frances Lester Warner, whose class was a joy. So also was Olive Hazlett's[2] class in the required freshman mathematics course. This brilliant young professor loved mathematics and conveyed her enthusiasm to some students by her blackboard demonstrations of complex problems. She surprised but elated me when after one class she said that mathematics should certainly be my major. In the mathematics courses taken in my sophomore and junior years, the professors, though competent, did not stimulate me as Miss Hazlett had done. This brilliant young woman soon left Mt. Holyoke for the University of Toronto.

Compared to freshman year, sophomore year was intellectually exciting. Laura Wild's required Bible class introduced us to the different sources behind the Old Testament books. The Hebrew leaders and prophets came alive, as she held forth on each. Although I was not a fundamentalist, some sophomores in the class seemed shocked by Miss Wild's scholarly approach to the Bible. The class in English Literature, taught by Mrs. Witcher, the wife of an Amherst professor, stands out in my memories. In our study of Shakespeare, each week a student wrote

2. "One of the two most noted women in America in the field of mathematics." Margaret Rossiter, *Women Scientists in America: Struggles and Strategies to 1940*, Johns Hopkins University Press, 1982, p. 174.

a one-page paper on some aspect of a play we had read and liked. Chemistry, however, was my favorite course that year: for the whole world of science, new to me, was opened by Miss Stevenson's lectures. I might have majored in it had I not in one of the early laboratory experiments broken a $10 glass beaker, whose replacement meant the loss of two months' allowance. Moreover, since it was the formulas and theories of chemistry which fascinated me rather than the laboratory, I assumed I was not cut out to be a chemist. At that time no counselling service existed where I might have been advised that science could be pursued even by a student who was not too good a technician.

My growing interest in world affairs led me in junior year (1920–21) to become a history–political science major. Mathematics remained as my minor. No longer can I possibly do a problem in the mathematical theory of probabilities; but because of that course I understand the reasoning back of the conventional bidding in bridge, long a favorite pastime. The course with Professor Neilson in English history from 1485 to the present introduced me to legal material. The legal steps in Henry VIII's break from Rome engaged my interest even more than the story of Henry and his six wives. In the seventeenth century the brilliant legal defense Strafford made in his trial moved me to tears. Since law and legal principles had become fascinating, I took a political science course in international law. My favorite course in political science was the history of political theory, especially since that class, taught by Professor Ellen Ellis, consisted of three truly interested seniors. Here we engaged in lively discussions of Plato, Machiavelli, Hobbes, etc. Once or twice I had the temerity to challenge the interpretation of our excellent professor, and I doubt whether she liked to have her approach questioned.

In junior year I was asked to write each day on a college post-office blackboard the headlines from the *New York Times*—particularly those concerning international events. In senior year Miss Neilson started an international relations club, where about twenty interested students met in the evening once a month.

In the spring of 1922, Irene Glascock and I were chosen as Mt. Holyoke delegates to attend a week-end conference on international affairs at Vassar. Was this possibly the first conference a women's college had sponsored on international affairs? To get to Vassar it was necessary to go by train to New York and stay overnight at a hotel. Dean Purington secured a room for us at the Martha Washington—as the safest place for "young ladies." Irene Glascock, our class poet, who tragically died soon after graduating and whose name has been perpetuated in an annual poetry contest, was more imaginative and adventurous than I. Rather than eating dinner in the sedate Martha Washington, she suggested we dine at the Astor, where I was entranced by the glitter and glory of New York. If my memory is correct, we went after dinner to my first New York play. Would Dean Purington have approved of our evening on the town? It is this evening, however, I most remember, for the conference at Vassar remains largely a blur in my mind, interested though I had become in international relations. A Vassar professor, Eloise Ellery, led the conference, but I have no recollections of the speakers or the topics discussed.

Until well into my junior year I lacked confidence in the scholastic ability I seemed to have. At mid-years in freshman year, waiting nervously to take my first *college* exam, I recall wondering whether I could meet the requirements of college. By junior year my confidence in myself had grown. Nevertheless, I was not prepared when Professor Young, the faculty head of the table on which I waited, asked me to come to her room after dinner. Expecting to be reproved (and rightly) for being at times a careless and absent-minded waitress, I was surprised when she told me that I had been one of the four juniors elected to Phi Beta Kappa. The formal announcement of the elections took place next day in chapel.

As senior year was drawing to a close, the inevitable question of what to do next arose. Since high-school teaching didn't attract me, how else could I earn my living? After much soul-searching and honest questioning of myself, I admitted that I loved learning and discussing ideas and hoped it might be possible to teach in a college. Fortunately Mt. Holyoke granted me a fellowship, and again my father, still a poor minister, provided the remaining funds for my first year at Radcliffe. In succeeding years I managed on my own, with fellowships from Radcliffe, tutoring history, coaching athletics in a summer camp, and teaching full-time in 1923/4 and 1924/5 and from 1928 to 1931.

To return to Mt. Holyoke. During my years there Mary Woolley became an international figure, going to Japan during our junior year. We knew her mostly as the dignified, impressive president who led us in required daily chapel service. At times, however, she gave us, from her podium in chapel, down-to-earth friendly advice. Before mountain day, suddenly declared a holiday one lovely day in October, she admonished her girls to bury deep in the wood the eggshells and garbage left from our picnic lunch. Miss Woolley cared for the environment. She also possessed a human touch and once showed a delightful sense of humor to two sophomores. On a cold winter morning, my roommate and I, living in Sycamores and fearing we would be late for chapel, broke a college rule and jumped on the back of a passing horse-drawn pung on runners. When it reached the chapel, off we jumped—almost knocking down Miss Woolley on her way thither. "Good morning, Gladys and Margaret," she graciously said. How did she ever know the names of two sophomores?

In retrospect I realize how much the Mt. Holyoke students of my day and later owe to Miss Woolley, who brought so many fine scholars and teachers to the college. In history, English, economics, chemistry, physics, zoology, and other departments, the academic reputation of the college steadily grew. "That the strength of the college is as the strength of its faculty cannot be too often repeated," Miss Woolley wrote. Year after year she stressed the vital importance of securing and retaining "the best men and women in personality, character, training, and teaching ability."[3] In my years there ninety to ninety-five percent of the faculty was made up of women. Unfortunately, I did not take my one

3. Quoted from the article by Caroline Harrison (M.H. '35), "Mary Woolley's Formula: Faculty Strength =College Strength," *Mt. Holyoke Alumnae Quarterly*, Spring 1982.

Ready for the party, aged 7

Graduating from Mt. Holyoke, 1922

philosophy course with Professor Warbeck, a much beloved male professor, and was not too pleased with my one male professor in psychology. Mt. Holyoke at that time was a college for women and taught by women. Amazingly it never entered my mind that, in the outside world of the professions and business, well-qualified, good and even brilliant women faced obstacles and many closed doors because of their sex.

My own love of the outdoors and sports played an important part in the years at Mt. Holyoke. First base was the position I played on my class team in baseball, using a hard ball in outdoor play and a soft one indoors. Volleyball was new to me, but it was great fun, and I became a member of our class team. Tennis was another favorite activity, but best of all were skiing and skating.

In senior year I became the first president of the newly formed Outing Club suggested by Miss Neilson. She too loved to ski and skate: she could cut fancy figures on the ice and taught some of us to waltz. The Outing Club was a joint faculty–student organization. Viola Barnes of the history department arranged for a Northampton man to bring horses to the campus for those wishing to ride, and Charlotte D'Evelyn of the English department often led small groups of students on long country walks, astonishing and often exhausting them with her long

strides and her endurance. The club rented a Connecticut river cottage for weekend groups to enjoy; and I organized the first skating carnival on the
lower lake, where one evening a band from Holyoke, for the "princely sum" of $100, played as we
skated round and round. On Prospect Hill we built
a little jump for skiers. "What are those girls at
Mt. Holyoke doing?" an inquiring reporter from
the *New York Times* asked and then journeyed to
college to find out. To answer one of his queries, I
skied off our tiny jump several times, but fell once,
sprawling with arms and legs in all directions. My
pride was hurt when, alas, that picture was the one
shown in his article in the *Times*. At least I can
boast in 1984 that once my picture did appear in the
Times.

Although I was voted the most absent-minded
student in the class, I don't believe it was true. In
Llamarada, the senior book, however, the caption
under my picture read, "Despite her absent-mind-
edness, she at least hasn't mislaid the Outing Club,
but has helped to steer it, we hope, to permanence."[4]
Underneath the caption was a drawing of Pegasus,
the class animal, on skis.

4. The Outing Club still exists.

Radcliffe '23 and '26

BEFORE CLASSES STARTED in Cambridge even first-year graduate students in those days went for advice on their courses to Professor Charles Homer Haskins, dean of the Harvard Graduate School. Expecting to specialize in modern European history and international relations, I remember his bright blue eyes looking right at me as he explained that for any serious study in those areas it was necessary to read not only French and German (which I could), but also Spanish, Italian, and Russian. Since I did not want to spend years learning new languages (not my favorite subject), I returned to his office a few days later and told him that English history, particularly in the seventeenth century, was my major interest. He quietly remarked, "Weren't you the girl who planned to concentrate in modern history and international relations?"

In contrast to Mt. Holyoke, Harvard professors (obviously all male) taught all courses. Some graduate courses were given on the Harvard campus and open to both sexes. And some professors chose to repeat their Harvard undergraduate courses for girls on the Radcliffe campus. This arrangement was financially profitable for them. My courses taken there in 1922/3 and 1925/6 introduced me to new areas of knowledge and strengthened my desire to teach in college. At the same time I became aware for the first time of the obstacles a woman planning a professional career faced.

Yet my own outstanding Harvard professors never seemed to regard their women students as inferior or as not worthy of their best teaching. Even in my first year Professor Charles McIlwain agreed to take me on in a research course, in which, about once every two or three weeks, he met only with me at his home. He accepted the research topic *I* suggested —The Development of the Theory of Parliamentary Sovereignty from 1640 to 1649—and guided my research upon it in the Gay Collection of pamphlets of that period in the Widener Library. This topic fascinated me and ultimately became my doctoral thesis. Even in our conferences the first year, McIlwain treated me as an equal—a scholar like himself —often implying I knew about this or that. Most times I didn't, but I left the conference determined to find out about it. In the more formal courses taken with him—Constitutional History of Colonial America, Medieval England, and the History of Political Theory—it was the depth of his learning and his profound interest in the many aspects of the subject that amazed his students. Whether McIlwain was lecturing on Magna Carta or on Maisiglio of Padua's *Defensor pacis*, he loved the text of the document before him on the desk, and "like any person in love he wanted everyone to know how beautiful was the object of his affections."[1]

I also had the opportunity to work with Wilbur C. Abbot in his graduate seminar in eighteenth- and nineteenth-century English history. He also cared for his women students. How touched I was when I met him by chance in the Widener stacks, and he stopped to tell me that he liked my first seminar paper!

How fortunate I was to have taken Professor Haskins' course on the intellectual history of the Middle Ages! For two hours this brilliant man, often shaking with some disease, would lecture to a room packed with students. In later years I used every opportunity in teaching to talk of the amazing and widespread contributions of the Moslem world, in science, philosophy, art, etc., to our western culture, which for centuries lagged far behind that of the Moslems. Of the three examination questions I re-

1. Paraphrased and quoted from Barbara Tuchman, *Practicing History*, Alfred A. Knopf, 1981, p. 14. In her essay, Mrs. Tuchman, a Radcliffe undergraduate, cited McIlwain as one of her most admired professors.

member from graduate work, two were asked by Haskins. In the lecture course he asked for the "Name, author and title of the books to be found in a typical library in western Europe in 600, 700, 800 . . . to 1400." Until late in the eleventh century the number in France or England was small— then came the Moslem translations (themselves often translations from the Greek). How many Americans today (even the educated), acutely aware of our dependence on oil from Saudi Arabia, are aware of our cultural debt to Moslem countries?

Robert Lord also lectured to a large class in his course on French history from the fifteenth century to the French Revolution. Although we never knew or approached him personally, it was he himself (no graduate assistant) who corrected our quizzes, making helpful comments in the margins. From all my undergraduate and graduate courses, Lord's beautifully organized notes were the only ones I kept and used in my own teaching.

In 1922/3, Fred Merk, young, shy, and brilliant, told the girls in his course on American constitutional history from 1789 to the present that he was giving the Radcliffe girls a more difficult final examination than the one for the boys at Harvard. Aware that "conscientious girls" would certainly not read a newspaper published the same morning as the day of the exam, he asked us to make a decision on the

Supreme Court case announced that morning. When he himself came to collect our papers and we eagerly inquired about the Court's decision, my spirits fell, for I had not agreed with it. Seeing my disappointment, Merk quietly said, "Brandeis also dissented." Years later, when Professor Merk was still lecturing at Harvard and I was carrying on research there, he graciously invited me to join him and other professors of history for lunch.

In retrospect, I realize how fortunate I was to have done graduate work at a time when I could study under so many of the truly "great" English and European history professors and scholars at Harvard. They did not—as far as I know—shortchange their women students.

During the two years spent at Radcliffe, much of my reading and research was done at Widener, the university library. Here, even as a first-year graduate student, I had a stall (shared with another person) in the stacks. The amount and wealth of the material on the numerous shelves devoted to English history amazed me—not only the older and latest books in every period and aspect of English history, but primary sources—state papers, local records from the counties, memoirs, etc. To wander from aisle to aisle amidst the abundance of this material was an education in itself. When by chance I came upon Tawney's *Religion and the Rise of Capitalism*, of which I had been ignorant, I put aside required work until I had finished this thought-provoking book.

It is true that the stacks in the Widener Library were closed to women after six o'clock, because the authorities claimed that women students might be raped in these narrow, long, often deserted dark corridors. Whether women could even enter the Harvard Law Library in the twenties I seriously doubt.

The only hater of scholarly women I ever personally encountered was Roger Merriman, who never in my day allowed a woman into his Harvard classes nor would condescend to repeat a course for girls at Radcliffe. Since Merriman taught the Renaissance and Reformation, one of the five fields required for my oral predoctoral general examination, McIlwain suggested I ask Merriman for some bibliography in this field. At his office in the Widener Library, during his office hours, I timidly knocked at the door. Half opening the door and seeing a woman outside, he kept one foot firmly planted beside the door, and quickly slammed it in my face, only taking time to say, "I never have anything to do with women." True to his word, fortunately for me, he did not examine me in the orals, but sent a lesser light in the Renaissance-Reformation field to question me.

In less spectacular ways I first came to realize at Radcliffe some of the pitfalls women scholars faced. Prior to the two-hour oral general examination required of Ph.D. candidates came a three-hour written exam. When I looked at the questions from which I discovered I must choose only one, my heart sank and I almost panicked, for none of the questions related more than partially to the fields I was offering. For one hour I struggled to decide which question to try to answer; then for the remaining two hours I pulled myself together and, mustering all the knowledge I had, wrote on "The significance and influence in ecclesiastical history and political thought of the Conciliar movement in the fifteenth century."

This experience in the written exam helped to make me especially nervous when I entered President Comstock's office, in which the oral exam was to be held. As a gracious gesture the professors had arranged that tea be served before the exam, and as a woman of course I was asked to pour. Three times Professor Haskins handed his cup of tea back to me, saying, "*Weaker* please, Miss Judson." Though I passed both the written and the oral exam, I'm sure I didn't cover myself with glory. Believing I would do well in political theory, I actually handled William Yandel Elliot's questions poorly. I later realized that the young Elliot cared more

about impressing his older colleagues as he conducted his first doctoral exam than about discover-
ing that I really knew something. Unfortunately,
although McIlwain was away that semester, I went
ahead with my orals. How I wish he had been one
of the examiners! Prior to the exam, the field I had
felt least confident about was French history from
1500 to 1789. Here, however, Professor Abbot, the
examiner in that subject, knew and liked me and
asked the kind of sweeping questions, moving from
century to century, which he knew I should be able
to answer. Fortunately I could, and somewhat re-
deemed myself.

Inspiring as McIlwain was in my work with him,
in practical matters—such as the job market, particularly for women scholars in the twenties and
thirties—he must have naïvely assumed that any
well-trained and good woman scholar would have
no problem in securing a position in a women's
college. At that time there were very few women
professors in co-educational universities, and none,
as far as I know, in men's colleges. Although I'm
sure he wrote the Radcliffe placement office about
me, he never, unlike Notestein at Yale, made personal efforts to interest history departments in other
colleges in his women graduate students. How little,
however, a few frustrations counted in comparison

with the value I received! My graduate work at Radcliffe and Harvard under such outstanding professors built firm and lasting foundations for my future profession.

Learning to Teach

IN 1924/5, as an assistant at Mt. Holyoke, I taught
the Renaissance-Reformation course—a period
(alas) in which I had never taken a course myself.
This performance was a pedantic, uninspired one,
with too much detail on the political history of the
separate Italian city-states and too little on the culture, particularly the art. Years later, finding among
my papers a lecture given that year entitled "*Final
solution of Erasmus,*" I was amazed at such a naïve
approach to any human being, let alone to a man as
complex as Erasmus.

In September 1928 I went as an instructor to the
New Jersey College for Women. Until 1918, when
the first class entered N.J.C., there had been no
liberal arts college for women in New Jersey. The
movement to establish such a college had started,
however, in 1911, initiated by the New Jersey State
Federation of Women's Clubs and the imaginative,
vigorous president of the College Club of Jersey
City, Mrs. Mable Smith Douglass. Where it should
be located, whether it should be independent or

affiliated with Rutgers, how it should be financed, and who should be the faculty, were time-consuming controversial problems which finally were resolved. The New Jersey Federation of Women's Clubs, sparked by Mrs. Douglass, persisted during these seven years to bring their hopes to fruition. Some Rutgers trustees opposed or seriously questioned the idea of a women's college, but James Neilson, Lenore F. Loree, and Dury Cooper, among others, supported it, as did Elmer Boyd, owner and editor of the New Brunswick *Home News*. Finally, in April 1918, a resolution was passed "that the Trustees of Rutgers College do establish a Women's College as a department of the state university of New Jersey maintained by the Trustees."[1] In September 1918 the first class of fifty-four students came to N.J.C. to "lead the way" in this new venture for the women of New Jersey.

Ten years later when I came, here was a college which had experienced an extraordinary growth. Its student body numbered 1,023. Numerous buildings providing classrooms and laboratories, dormitories and a central dining-hall, had been built, scattered from Gibbons Campus and Antilles Field on

1. Trustees' minutes, April 12, 1918; Frelinghuysen to Demarest, February 16, 1918. For further details see George P. Schmidt, *Douglass College: A History*, Rutgers University Press, 1968; and Richard P. McCormick, *Rutgers: A Bicentennial History*, Rutgers University Press, 1966.

the Raritan to the Jameson and Douglass campuses and the Little Theater on Nichol Avenue. The beautiful Vorhees Chapel graced the original campus, and in September 1928 I attended the dedication of the newly built music building, given by the New Jersey Women's Clubs. (No more buildings were constructed until 1953, although a separate library and new gymnasium were sorely needed.)

In the early twenties, Rutgers professors taught most of the courses, but Dean Douglass gradually replaced them with N.J.C. faculty of her own choice. Alumnae of that period still speak fondly of their Rutgers professors: Dicky Morris in mathematics, Irving Kull in history, and Whitman in literature are the names I hear mentioned most frequently.

An innovative department of student life had been created, and an honor system for student offenses, academic and social, worked (for the most part). By 1928 loyal alumnae were already praising and supporting their alma mater, happy to have participated in this decade of growth.

As a college within Rutgers University, N.J.C. could honor its best students with a Phi Beta Kappa key. The American Association of University Women, however, would not accept this new women's college as one of its members. It insisted, so I was told, that the faculty must include more women professors. Accordingly, in 1927 Mrs. Douglass brought in Professors Emily Hickman in history, Shirley Smith in classics, and Helen Hazen in home economics. For the next twenty to thirty years, these women, in addition to their teaching and departmental work, contributed much to faculty and committee work and discussions. A story circulates that after Mrs. Douglass satisfied the A.A.U.W. with the appointment of those three women professors, she remarked, "Now I will bring in some handsome men." Whether or not the story is true I have no idea, but the tenured professors brought in for a number of years *were* men, some of them handsome.

Whether Mrs. Douglass chose a handsome man or woman professor or a lowly instructor, she seriously considered each possible new member of the N.J.C. faculty. In my spring interview for the position of instructor, Dean Douglass entertained me alone for lunch, and must have decided I met her requirements, whatever they were. I was brought in to replace the Rutgers professor who had taught English history; but in September 1928, upon arriving in New Brunswick, I was told that I must teach, not English history, but a junior-senior course in Europe from 1870 to the present. Although never asked as to my competence to teach such a course, I was fortunately slightly more qualified to handle it than my Renaissance-Reformation one earlier at Mt. Holyoke.[2] Nevertheless, the midnight oil frequently burned as I struggled to disentangle the complexities of the Balkans and the confused diplomacy leading to World War One. The seniors in that class looked so wise, particularly Patsy Collins Hunter and Rosamund Sawyer Moxon. Could I have looked into a crystal ball and seen that later Patsy would be executive secretary of the college and Rosamund chairman of the Rutgers board of trustees, I would have been even more scared than I was. Both of these impressive seniors told me later that they were also scared of me, and thought I demanded a lot of work from them. In 1966, however, Patsy wrote that I was the "best teacher" she ever had, and Roz "remembered and rejoiced in that class of 1928/29." For six or seven years I continued to give this course. To study Bismarck, the background of World War One, President Wilson and the unfortunate Treaty of Versailles, the Russian Revolution, and the utopian hopes of the twenties to bring about a more peaceful world, was an experience I have never regretted, and I am glad to have been assigned to this course. Today, in this age

2. In 1923/24 I had taught mathematics at the Buckingham School in Cambridge for $1600, because, although history was the subject in which I had my M.A., $1200 was the best salary offered me for teaching high-school history.

With a group of faculty and friends in the thirties

Opening a discussion on liberal arts education in 1950
(l. to r.: Agnes Townsend, Dorothy Nelson, Margaret Judson, Frances Bickelhaupt Wilcox, Marguerite Richards)

With Jean Sidar in the early sixties

when a historian is trained and hired as a specialist in, for example, some aspect of American colonial, or pre– or post–Civil War, social history, it would be unthinkable to ask him to teach American diplomatic history.

Until 1962/3 the Douglass department remained a joint history–political science one, which was excellent and innovative. In the thirties, six members had Ph.D.s (four in history, two in political science) while a joint department in Arts and Science (now Rutgers College) had three (one in history, two in political science).[3] Aware of the growing importance of the East to the United States, Dr. Emily Hickman, although no specialist in the field, gave a course on the history of Japan and China. Her course in European intellectual history from 1500 to the present is still remembered by alumnae, many of them not history majors. Today Rutgers University offers numerous courses in American social and intellectual history, but in the thirties Dr. George Schmidt's course in American Society was the first offered in the university. Dr. Anna Campbell had her scholarly book on *The Black Death and Men of Learning* published almost forty years before *The Tumultuous Century* by Barbara Tuchman. She also offered, although again no specialist in the field,

3. Two instructors in political science, here for a year or two, also had Ph.D.s.

a course on the Moslem world and its history. My course in Tudor-Stuart England gave the students the opportunity to work in a limited period and, though undergraduates, to learn to use many primary sources. In political science Dr. Mildred Moulton's course in welfare problems of government drew many devoted students to whom she opened up a new world. Dr. Harold Van Dorn's book *Twenty Years of the Chinese Republic: Two Decades of Progress* was published as early as 1932.

No wonder Dr. Schmidt could hardly believe a rebuff of this excellent department received from the chairman of Arts and Science's education department. When during World War Two Dr. Schmidt suggested that one or more members of his department teach in the Rutgers University summer school, he was told they were not qualified, since Douglass professors were "only inflated high-school teachers."

Each of the older members of the highly respectable Douglass department welcomed its newest member, treating her as an equal in the department, and inviting her to their homes with colleagues in other departments. Naturally, the chairman was a man, George Schmidt, but a man who respected his women colleagues, treating us as equals. Under his quiet but wise guidance, we generally achieved a consensus in department meetings. And how tactfully he handled the three women prima donnas in the department in the thirties (I wasn't one of them)! When the split between history and political science came (because in the rest of the university history and political science had long been separate departments), the division into two departments at Douglass was a friendly, mutually arranged one. For years members of our joint department had lived happily together, each discipline benefiting, I believe, from the heated but stimulating department discussions which were carried on.

For a number of years—until the early seventies—History I and II was a required course at Douglass. The policy of our department for many years was that each member from full professor to instructor would teach one or more sections of freshman history. What to include or omit in the course was of major concern in our department meetings. Margaret Hastings lingered in the Middle Ages, I in the Renaissance-Reformation period, while Emily Hickman galloped through those periods to reach the present situation and problems of the contemporary world. Once when she was asked how she reached the French Revolution so soon, she calmly replied, "Oh, I omitted the church in the Middle Ages." Undoubtedly many freshmen would not have chosen the course had it been voluntary, for too often the teachers of history in high school did

not have the same degree of knowledge or of training for teaching their subject as the teachers of
mathematics or science or language had. Nor had I
any training for teaching contemporary civilization
to freshmen. Faced with three sections of freshman
history for several years (and one section even in
1966), I taught myself, step by step, or year by year,
to make this required course of value and interest to
as many students as possible, whatever their future
majors might be.

Each professor of this introductory course has his
or her own way of handling the material. What
came to be mine? Naturally and unconsciously I
believe I conveyed my own love of history to some
members of the class, hoping to share it with them.
Whatever the subject taught—history, mathematics,
chemistry, language—some students at least (never
all) feel the spark which an enthusiastic teacher ig-
nites. Invariably the first question a freshman asked
this instructor in History One was, "Do we have
to remember many dates?" Many can be eliminated
or approximated, I assured them, but since history is
an account of man, his institutions, and activities,
his ideas and his culture, moving through time, this
story requires some dates or pegs to hang upon.

Particularly in a survey course, *selectivity* is vital.
There never is enough time to deal adequately with
so many subjects. Yet somehow I tried hard to dis-

pel the deep-seated notion that all the Middle Ages were the Dark Ages, to arouse their enthusiasm for the great artists of the Italian Renaissance, and to grasp the basic issues, drama, and significance of the Protestant Revolt. Somehow in this course the great scientific achievements of western civilization and their impact on our thinking, as well as on our lives, must be made more than names and dates to freshmen, and the complexity of international problems and attitudes leading to World War One be explained without completely confusing the students.

They should come to realize that for history, as for science, facts are essential; but important also are the questions asked, some of which can be answered, and others not, even by the professor. Historians are supposed, of course, to know everything. One freshman had read in the text discussing the medieval church that the pope was elected by the college of cardinals and the Holy Ghost. And who was the Holy Ghost? she asked me in class. Another student seemed disillusioned when I couldn't answer to her satisfaction all her questions about the love-life and mistresses of Charles II. The questions I liked best from students, whether freshmen or graduates, were those which made me aware that I hadn't given thought to the particular problem the student was raising, or which gave me new insights and approaches to the topic under consideration. One of my freshman classes seemed surprised when told that a particular student, whose written work fell between grades A and B, received an A in the course because of the thoughtful questions she asked in class.

The instructor should be flexible enough to adjust her prepared plan for the hour to the unexpected. Perhaps the most effective freshman class I ever had was unexpectedly taught by a student. As I was about to embark on Hitler's policies in Germany leading to the holocaust, suddenly I thought it possible that one of the freshmen sitting in that class might herself have experienced them in Nazi Germany. She had, and she held the class spellbound as she told how the authorities had entered her home at night and arrested her parents.

Well aware of the fact that much of what the freshmen had learned in my course on contemporary civilization would be forgotten even while they were still in college, I hoped that (at least) some of them had become aware of an educated person's need for history. I treasure the remark one student made about my class (whether she intended it as a compliment or as a criticism) that "Miss J. expects us to think."

With all my aspirations for the freshmen, it was sobering to realize that with some I failed completely. In one class a prospective gym major sat in the front and yawned or slept most of the time. After enduring her behavior too long, I asked her to stay after class. "Since nothing I or a book can do," I told her, "can interest you in history, will you please sit in the last row of seats for your morning or afternoon nap?" Somehow moved by this approach, she followed the spirit of my request and aroused herself enough to pass the course. When we met on campus in later years before and after she graduated, she often stopped for a friendly chat with me.

I learned that at least one freshman had complained at home about her history professor. It was a Douglass custom for the faculty who taught freshmen to meet, talk, and have tea with their freshmen and their parents in the auditorium of the music building on an October Sunday afternoon. The first freshman, with her parents in tow, whom I met one such afternoon, was one of the poorest in that class. As I rose to the occasion and greeted her and her parents, her father, looking right at me, remarked, "She can't be the ogre you've complained about, for she has nice blue eyes."

Yes, teaching a required freshman course in contemporary civilization is quite an experience. It is harder to plan and teach such a survey than a more advanced one or a graduate seminar. If possible, full professors should teach it sometimes too, for their own education as well as the freshmen's. In retrospect I am happy to have had this opportunity for many years, and I was sorry that in my first two or three years of retirement the laws of New Jersey prevented me from working even part-time, for I would have liked to teach such an introductory course at nearby Middlesex Junior College.

Three Advanced Courses

FOR ABOUT TWENTY-FIVE YEARS, from 1940 to 1965, I taught three junior–senior courses in fields of my own choice—Tudor-Stuart England, the Renaissance and the Reformation, and the History of Political Thought. Only two of these were given in any one year. What were some of my objectives and techniques in each of these courses?

In Tudor-Stuart England I deliberately chose to concentrate on some periods in considerable detail, necessarily having to skim over others more superficially. For example, the period from 1529 through 1536, when England severed its ties with Rome, provided the opportunity for history majors to study the *complexity* of forces resulting in the break from Rome. The part played by Henry and his wives, particularly Catherine of Aragon, by Cardinal Wolsey and Thomas Cromwell, his principal ministers, by Thomas Cranmer, his religious supporter, and Thomas More, the friend who finally defied him; the step-by-step pressure the government put upon the English clergy to accept the change; the indispensable part played by Parliament and its statutes in legalizing and enforcing the break; the dilemma faced by the pope, coerced by Charles V: here in a few years perhaps the most dramatic and significant changes in English history took place. At hand in the Douglass and Rutgers libraries were collections of primary sources which all the students used on some topic. One student, using the Letters and Papers of Henry VIII, wrote an excellent paper on the propaganda set forth by the government to justify its actions. Years later a librarian in the Alexander Library thanked me for her first introduction to primary sources in that undergraduate course.

This course gave the students an opportunity to feel somewhat at home in a past age. I did my best to help them shed their twentieth-century attitudes when dealing, for example, with Puritans. They certainly were surprised when I suggested that, if the American students protesting against the Vietnam war had lived in Elizabethan or Caroline England, many would have been angry and protesting Puritans.

Although constitutional issues and ideas in the seventeenth century are the subject of my own publications, it is much harder to teach the Stuart century than the Tudor. Except for Charles II, no

Stuart monarch is glamorous. I regret that only after my retirement did I become really interested in Charles I. When teaching the pre–civil war period I concentrated on Parliament and failed to treat Charles I's own part adequately. Since retirement, my research upon him has made me realize that, but for his ideas and attitudes, his maneuvers, his manipulations, his mistakes, and his choice of councillors, the civil war might well have not taken place. My research notes gathered upon Charles I still exist. In the last two or three years younger scholars have delivered papers which bring out some of the same points as are included in my own notes. Naturally I regret that because of declining energy it became impossible to do further research upon Charles which might have resulted in publication.

If I failed in my own teaching to deal adequately with Charles' part in bringing on the civil war, fortunately I believe I came to do Cromwell justice. In the winter of '55, when working in London on a Guggenheim Fellowship, I was forced to spend several days in bed because of a flu-like cold. The only books at hand to read happened to be the three volumes of Carlyle's *Cromwell*, which I had just purchased. Although I had taught Cromwell for many years, I now came to know him much better, after spending three days in bed with him reading his letters and speeches. Henceforth in teaching him,

I chose selected sections from Carlyle or Abbot's volumes and from the Putney Debates for the students to read and discuss in class. Whether students liked or disliked him, after Cromwell himself spoke to them, was immaterial, but all of them, as far as I know, came to understand better the kind of man he was—both revolutionary and conservative—and the agonizing decisions he faced—whether to execute Charles, to dissolve the Rump, to refuse the Crown offered him, etc.

The best short essay I know on Cromwell is in G. M. Trevelyan's *Autobiography and other essays*.[1] This essay is entitled *Cromwell's Statue*, "which was not hidden away during the Second World War, but remained under fire, guarding the entrance of the House of Commons, with Bible and Sword" (p. 158). The students read this essay and liked it. The Tudor-Stuart class in 1950 presented me with the book, writing on the fly page, "To a stimulating and sympathetic teacher"—a gift and tribute I treasure.

It is impossible (I believe) to convey to students or anyone else in *one* lecture the man Cromwell and his part in the turmoil of England in his day. In History I and II, when occasional lectures were given by different members of the department to all sec-

1. London, 1949.

tions of Contemporary Civilization, naturally the lecture on Cromwell fell to me. I'll never know whether or not some few freshmen might, under normal circumstances, have become interested in him, for the lecture was scheduled and given on the Monday in November 1963 after John Kennedy had just been shot. Neither the students nor their professor cared about Cromwell that morning as I did my best to struggle through that lecture.

For over twenty years I taught "A Study of Leading Political Thinkers and Significant Political Ideas." As the course description indicates, not only were major political philosophies, beginning with Plato and concluding in the nineteenth century with Hegel, Marx, and John Stuart Mill, read and discussed, but also basic political concepts shaping our western political world. This approach to the course would undoubtedly be questioned by a philosophy professor or by some contemporary political scientist concerned with computers and models. I believe, however, that this approach was of value not only to history and political science majors but also to the considerable number of students with a variety of other majors—ranging from chemistry to art. Their participation in the class widened our discussions. Although at times I lectured, for the most part the students first read Plato's *Republic*, Aris-

totle's *Politics*, or Hobbes' *Leviathan* before hearing
any comments from me. How they understood and
reacted to a thinker led into the class discussion
and my own remarks. To me it seemed important
that they grasp what the thinker was saying before
they launched into a violent criticism of him. Plenty
of opportunity was provided, later, for criticism,
arguments, and disagreements among the students
and between them and the professor. Invariably,
about half of the students came to prefer Plato's
Republic to Aristotle's *Politics*.

The other advanced course I taught for a number
of years was the Renaissance and Reformation. In
contrast to my overemphasis on the political when
I first taught the subject at Mt. Holyoke in 1924/5,
my increasing interest in and knowledge of Italian
art and humanist ideas were now woven into the
course. The Renaissance had come alive for me—
and I believe it did so for many of my students. No
longer did my notes contain the "Final solution of
Erasmus."

In teaching Luther, I made sure that his own
writings were studied and discussed as they revealed
the approach this essentially medieval man took
while he examined his own conscience and, step by
step, questioned basic Catholic teachings. How and
why his ideas caught fire in Germany in the early

sixteenth century, the confusion, and even revolt, resulting in German society after he stood firm at Worms—these provided the opportunity for students to watch and understand the interplay of revolutionary ideas in a traditional society. Although not a Roman Catholic, I worked hard to present fairly the Catholic reaction and response to the Protestant successes. Much later one member of a class told me that after graduation she had become a convert to Roman Catholicism, but that the instructor in the faith had told her she needed no instruction as she had learned the essentials in her college Renaissance-Reformation course.

For one semester I gave for the first time a senior seminar for history majors. Here the students read and discussed different kinds of historians, including (among others) Thucydides, Bede, Voltaire, Carlyle, Bancroft, Ranke, and Bloch. Each student wrote a paper on a historian dealing with a period which she had not studied in a formal course.

In each of the advanced courses taught I prepared a list of the most important topics to be treated, and of the required and the suggested reading for several weeks. At the end of each class I also indicated the probable topics for the next class. The girls had generally done some of the required reading before

57

the class discussion of it. When, however, a number of Rutgers boys took the Renaissance-Reformation course, and I suggested they should have done that much of the reading, a chorus of loud guffaws sounded. Eventually most of the boys did some reading before the class, as they discovered that their irrelevant questions and comments were not appreciated in our class discussions.[2] Normally a class consisted of student discussion of specific material with comments and mini-lectures by me interpolated at the right moment during the class. When occasionally I gave a formal lecture, it dealt with material where no suitable reading existed and it was necessary to cover that subject. In my preparation for a class, I almost always read some new article or book on the subject, injecting some of the points made in it into my remarks or lecture. In that way, I myself felt fresh and stimulated to teach that topic again. In each of these three advanced courses, a student prepared and reported on some topic or participated in a panel presentation of a subject.

During my many years here, I think I did slowly develop my ability to teach. When in 1962 I re-

2. When the boys in this class heard of the dinner my junior-senior students were to give for me in 1966, when I expected to retire, the department secretary told me that boys in this class called to be included at the dinner. I was touched by the especially designed silver pin given me, inscribed on the back "to M.A.J. in appreciation."

ceived a Linbach award for distinguished teaching, Dean Ruth Adams, who had recommended me, told me that in her talks with alumnae in different parts of New Jersey many of them had spoken enthusiastically of their classes with me. In my early years, Emily Hickman, an outstanding teacher, encouraged me to inject student discussion into my classes and not rely on straight lecturing. I also owed much to my friend Jessica Linneman who, as a psychologist and student counsellor, made me more aware of the role human beings play in history. Although my published research dealt with ideas in their historical setting,[3] I wish I had been able to write a biography of some person. My teaching at least was enriched by Jessica's understanding of people.

3. I regret that my hope and plan of writing as an *older woman* an essay upon the *older* Queen Elizabeth did not materialize.

Religious Heritage

ONE OF THE MOST interesting and challenging courses in which I played an important part was "The Religious Heritage of Western Civilization," which was written up in the *Christian Science Monitor* of May 12, 1951.

Influence of Man's Religious Yearnings
On Western Thought Explored by Students

A three-year-long experiment in teaching and in learning is under way at New Jersey College for Women—a course called "The Religious Heritage of Western Civilization." So rich and rewarding an experience has it proved to be that its status as an experiment seems likely to change to one of permanence in the college curriculum.

For the faculty it has broken down the usual subject-matter boundaries and brought about a new inter-departmental teaching project, with shared responsibilities. For the students it has provided a cultural theme broader and more inclusive than normally attempted in any other course. It has offered upperclassmen an opportunity to deal with a comprehensive subject in a mature way.

UNIFYING THEME

"Religious History 391–392," as it is prosaically labeled in the catalogue of the woman's college of Rutgers University, weaves together the different threads from which our religious heritage is drawn: religious expression in literature, art, music, philosophy, and social institutions.

Religion is the underlying theme that carries through all the lectures—the motivating force and the unifying factor. But it is treated very broadly, since the main aim of the course is to give students an understanding of the important part that religion has played in our cultural heritage.

Obviously no one professor can deal authoritatively with all of these subjects, so a cooperative teaching method was chosen, drawing upon members of the art, languages, music, history, philosophy, and other departments.

A student who elects "Religious Heritage" learns from not one but 15 or more professors. She finds the variety of presentation makes the material more interesting, that new ideas flourish from different interpretations.

One week the class may hear Professor of Art Robert Bradshaw lecture on "The Religious Heritage of Medieval Art," illustrated by numerous slides of paintings, sculpture, and architecture of that period.

The following week they move to the music department where Professor of Music Duncan McKenzie discusses "The Religious Heritage of Medieval Music," using the piano or instrumental recordings to make his points.

Throughout the year lectures and discussions cover such subjects as "Amos and Social Justice," "Dante's Divine Comedy," "New England Puritans," and "The Social Philosophy of the Catholic and Protestant Churches Today."

Students learn of the relationship between religion and contemporary political thought from a professor of political science. Or, another week, discuss religion as related to natural science with a physics professor.

Dr. Margaret Judson, Professor of History, acts as coordinator of the course. Present at every class, she helps the students tie together all the material in discussion and review periods. She also takes part in the actual teaching by lecturing in her own field of history.

Student reaction to "Religious Heritage" has been encouraging. The enrollment has doubled since the course was initiated in 1948. Open only to juniors and seniors, it has drawn students from all major fields of study.

Their comments, on the whole, have been favorable. This semester several have said, "The course synthesizes the contributions of diverse fields and clarifies ideas previously held." "It has opened up entire new vistas of thought." "I like the idea of meeting many new professors—it creates a variety of outlook and approach, which keeps the course fresh and alive all year long."

MUTUAL BENEFITS

The course has overcome one practical obstacle that might well doom any elective subject. Classes must be held Monday, Wednesday, and Friday, during the very last period of the day. But instead of making the course a small one, enrollment rose—some students recommended longer class hours and more time for discussion.

Obviously, the tremendous scope of the course has been a stimulating challenge. Primarily a matter of individual study and responsibility, the subject demands that students go to original sources and dip into fields of thought seldom touched in other courses.

But the benefits are not all on the student side. Participating faculty members have found it an enlightening experience. Because the teacher must approach his own field from an entirely different angle to relate it to the central theme, many have discovered fresh viewpoints on old familiar subjects.

Its major importance, according to Dr. Judson, is that "through this study, upperclass students at the State University gain a better knowledge and understanding of religion in general. The course helps them to view more objectively and tolerantly religious ideas other than their own. It makes them realize, as perhaps they had not before, that religion has been and still is a potent and dynamic factor in western civilization. Through contact with the original works of writers and artists deeply concerned with religion, students gain new insights into the religious struggles and achievements—the beliefs and aspirations—of man in his long history."

As a supplement to this excellent article written by the reporter from Boston who came to New Brunswick to learn of the course, I will add that

the students were impressed by the fact that Neil
McDonald, a professor of political science, gave the
lecture on the Ten Commandments; Henry Winkler,[1] a Rutgers professor of history and a Jew, the
one on the social teachings of Amos; Fred Rockwell
from the English department the one on the Psalms;
William Norton, the philosophy professor, the one
on Aquinas; Emiliana Noether, an Italian Catholic and history professor, the one on Dante; George
Schmidt, a history professor educated at a Lu-
theran seminary, the one on Luther; Manuel Salas,
a Spanish professor, the one on St. Theresa;
and Wilfred Jackson, a physics professor, those on
Jesus and on the relation between science and religion in the contemporary world. From outside the
university, Professor John Beardsley of the New
Brunswick Theological Seminary lectured on St.
Paul, a man about whom he had expert knowledge.
In addition we secured a Jesuit priest and scholar
from New York who talked on the theology of the
early Christian church. As for myself, I not only
lectured in my special field—the English Puritans,
for example—but whenever an important theologian,
such as St. Augustine, had to be treated and no one
else was willing to tackle it. The students were
amazed that so many professors from different

1. Now president of the University of Cincinnati.

fields cared to talk to them on a subject concerned with religion. However well a single professor of religion might have taught the course, the impact upon the students would, I believe, have then been less valuable.

Since the professors involved met with me to plan the different parts of the course, we all benefited from our discussions on whom and what to include. A successful cooperative course needs cooperative planning.[2]

How did this course come into existence? Until 1955/6 there was no department of religion at Douglass, although the Reverend Everard Deems of the Baptist church in New Brunswick had given one or two courses on the Douglass campus, and Professor Fales, of the Arts and Science sociology department, one on the Bible. Dean Corwin therefore formed a committee to consider the need for more academic courses involving religion at Douglass. As a member of the committee, I suggested this course on our western religious heritage. Unfortunately, this cooperative experimental course did not become a permanent one in the Douglass curriculum. It certainly was successful, as the *Christian Science Monitor* article states, and I can add that alumnae returning to college spoke to me frequently

2. The *New York Times* in 1982 spoke of the value of the "new" trend in cooperative teaching.

about that particular course. As so often happens, its discontinuation resulted from lack of money. As its coordinator, I was able to include it as one of the four courses I taught (each of the other three was a different course). But although this arrangement did not inconvenience me, we were troubled that nothing could be done for the other professors, who gave their services to the course in addition to performing their regular heavy duties. Most of the professors lectured only once or twice, but Professor Bradshaw in art many times. Although he would have continued to lecture, his participation should certainly have been integrated into his already heavy schedule in the art department. It proved impossible, because of the shortage of money, for the administration and the art department to do so. Consequently it was (I believe) a group decision that the course should be dropped.

Letters from Students

PERHAPS THE GREATEST satisfaction and happiness for an older or retired professor come from the letters from those former students who tell you that your courses taken five to thirty years earlier are still remembered. When I received in 1962 the Linbach Award for distinguished teaching, or when in 1966 I "retired" and unexpectedly later that year became acting dean, it was heartwarming to receive a number of such letters. Most of them were from the best students, but not all. One who called herself an "undistinguished student" wrote, "There have been teachers who have cluttered up their classrooms with themselves and their histrionics but quietly, gently, unassumingly you unrolled an age before your class and there it stood in all its glory."

This tribute pleased me as much as the most scholarly one, made by an outstanding male student in a graduate seminar who was later to become a professor of history. "The high standards which you set in this course have inspired me beyond the acquisition of knowledge about Tudor and Stuart England. I am particularly grateful for your own example of scholarly integrity, as well as your concern for thoroughness in research and acquiring a feeling for the primary sources."

An undergraduate student who went on to graduate school elsewhere wrote that, the more experience she had as a teacher herself, the "more admiration I have for the manner in which you structured your courses and presented the material. If, at the end of my career, I can say that I have honestly tried to live up to the example you set both as a scholar and a teacher, I will be content." To another student I "represented what a college professor should be and what a college-educated woman should strive to be."

A major in political science expressed her "unending appreciation for the insight you conveyed about the treasures of western political thought." Another political science major wrote:[1] "Political thought was the single most valuable subject I studied. I find daily as a bureaucrat that my confidence with the world of ideas and writing, my sense of history and my capacity for hope for the human enterprise have held me in good stead in troubled times—a credit to political thought!! and you."

A senior in the Renaissance-Reformation course,

1. In a letter written to me in June 1983 when I was in hospital after a heart attack.

planning to go to graduate school, wrote: "Your course was the most interesting and rewarding during my whole college career. . . . But what was most important for me was that you showed me how to treat material as a historian—to be aware of the full significance of a document or a date. . . . I will always remember the sparks that were always present in your class."

An English major in the class of 1964 wrote[2] concerning my Renaissance-Reformation course, "Although I was fortunate to study under a number of distinguished teachers during my Douglass career, I remember Dr. Judson as the most outstanding and inspiring of these dedicated men and women. . . . Her course offered something of interest to students in every discipline; the issues raised during classes stimulated long and heated dormitory discussions that took the course far beyond the classroom; the exams forced you to evaluate what you had studied and re-shape it into your own thought. Finally, the Socratic method Dr. Judson employed so effectively to elicit response and interest in the classrooms, combined with the enthusiasm and brilliance with which she tied together students' diverse opinions into a unified thesis at the end of each hour, provided a classic study in the art of teaching."

2. In a letter to Mary Hartman dated March 28, 1984, which she sent on to me.

Other former students thanked me for making the material "come alive, vital, and meaningful," conveying to them my devotion to and enthusiasm for history, "and showing me that history could be so alive and interesting." One student hoped "that I would find sustained joy in knowing the teaching part of my life's work raised the horizon for a naïve, unenlightened student." Another commented that "you certainly played a large part in helping me to obtain the true essence of an education," while a graduate student wrote, "You have truly made a mark in my career."

It was gratifying to learn that some students remembered me not only as teacher and scholar, but as a person. One student wrote that "you were the warmest, most wonderful professor I have had the privilege to know." Another thanked me "for the kindness you showed a stumbling, frightened student." The time had come, one excellent student wrote, to acknowledge how much I "as a scholar, a teacher, and a person have meant to me over the last twenty-five years—and will continue to mean."

In February 1983, the following letter came unexpectedly from an excellent student in the forties whom I had never seen since her graduation.

"I cannot ever tell you how important an influence you have been in my life. I learned from you intellectual discipline, intellectual honesty—and a deep and abiding love for history. More, I learned by your marvelous example that a woman should be as much as she can be—in whatever role. . . . You were the pre-eminent role model for the intellectual, dedicated, *humane* woman. . . . I will never forget the lovely person who was my favorite teacher."

When I was snatched from retirement to serve as acting dean, some students and faculty, unaware of my age, wished that I might serve in that capacity for several years. One student hoped that "you will be with us for many years, sharing your heart, your mind, and your grace."

Non-Classroom Activities
and Promotion

IN THE YEARS at Douglass (up to 1966/7), not only did practically all members of the faculty, both men and women, teach nine to twelve hours, but many (as well as the chairmen) counselled their own students and served on college and in some cases on university committees. In the thirties, as an assistant professor, I chaired the conference at Douglass, attended by representatives from a number of women's colleges, that informed high-school students about college in general. From 1940 to 1946 I was chairman of the joint faculty–student War Service Committee which coordinated and sponsored many activities, including teaching girls and faculty how to perform minor auto repairs. The committee organized the first (and perhaps best) faculty show to raise money for war relief,[1] and, perhaps most significantly, it sponsored lectures

1. See George Schmidt's book for further details.

every two weeks on the issues and progress of the war. Those lectures, some by outside speakers and others by Douglass faculty, generally filled the largest lecture room, particularly when Professor Hickman of our own history department gave the lecture. In 1943 *Quair*, the senior year book, was dedicated to me, with the following tribute: "To Dr. Margaret A. Judson, whose untiring activity has enabled our college to take its place in the war, and whose knowledge of the past and understanding of the present have turned our eyes to the great and solemn task the future holds, to a wise historian and inspiring humanitarian, we dedicate the 1943 *Quair*." I am most happy to be the honorary member of the N.J.C. class of 1943.

For a number of years in the thirties and forties, I also served on the Douglass Admission Committee, and, beginning in the late forties, for five or six years as chairman of the Educational Policy Committee. At no time was my teaching load reduced for committee responsibilities, nor did I expect it to be. As I will describe later, I carried on research during the summers of these years, and was granted a leave of absence for it in 1938/9 and in the second semester of 1946. In 1938/9 there was no university policy on research or funds available for it. By 1946, when the Rutgers Research Council had been founded, it provided funds for my salary.

Until at least 1940 a substantial majority of the department chairmen were men. Understandably, in physical education the chairman was a woman, Helena Keyes; in home economics, Helen Hazen; and in the N.J.C. Library School, Ethel Fair. Jane Inge was chairman of the department of speech and dramatic art, Jessie Feske of botany, Shirley Smith of classics, and Madame de Visme of French for a few years. In four departments—bacteriology, mathematics, philosophy and psychology, and physics—the members were all men. In two large departments, those of English and English literature and of music, there was only one woman.

As for salaries, at Douglass they were for the most part lower even for men than in Arts and Science (now Rutgers College) and still lower for women. As an instructor I started at $2,200, which was cut by 10% (also for men, I believe) during much of the thirties. When I became an associate professor in 1941 or '42, I think my salary was raised to $3,500. During the thirties, and until 1946, when my mother died, I was helping to support my parents. Since this help was less than one-half their support and they did not live in my home (an attic apartment without a real kitchen), I received no tax deduction for this support. In 1949, when I was forty-nine, Professor Schmidt recommended me for a full professorship. I had already published in a fest-

74

schrift for Professor McIlwain at Harvard, and *The Crisis of the Constitution* was in press. At the Douglass Appointments and Promotion Committee, however, the dean seemed to favor the promotion of a male English professor. Fortunately for me, however (as he later told me), Professor Schmidt on this committee, normally a gentle man, put his foot down. He insisted that he would not vote for the promotion of the English professor unless the committee would also vote to promote me to full professor—which they did. Without a man's help, I suspect I would not have been promoted at that time. As it turned out, I think I was the first woman at Douglass who came as an instructor and finally was promoted to full professor.[2]

During the depression years of the thirties, few women professors in any college moved elsewhere, as far as I know. As for myself, Professor Viola Barnes, chairman of the history department at Mt. Holyoke, had written me in the early forties practically offering me a position there. President Ham, I later learned, did not endorse her recommendation. And why? Not because of me, whom he never saw, but because he believed there had been and still were too many older women professors at the

2. In fairness to the long time I waited, I should say that "in the depression and war years" not too many promotions even for men were granted at Douglass.

college, and that any new appointment should be a young man, and not a young woman. Although I probably would have gone to Mt. Holyoke had the position been offered, I suspect in retrospect that my future years at Douglass and Rutgers opened up wider opportunities for me.

In the early forties, I was also offered the academic deanship at the Connecticut College for Women and told that when, in a few years, the president retired, I would if all went well become a strong candidate to succeed her. After wrestling for days with my decision, the answer was no, for a number of reasons—the most important being my desire to complete the research for and writing of *The Crisis of the Constitution*, and to continue to teach, both of which would have been too difficult, if not impossible, for an administrator.

The Berkshire
Historical Association

IN MAY 1929 OR '30, Emily Hickman took me to the second meeting of the Berkshire Historical Association. The year before,[1] a group of women historians had agreed to meet informally once a year to discuss their interests in history more fully than was possible at the December meeting of the American Historical Association. Over the years I attended at least 85 per cent of these spring meetings generally held in the Berkshires.

From the early thirties, who are some of the older historians that stand out in my mind? From Wellesley there came Mrs. Elizabeth Hodder and Judith Williams, whom I can still see sitting in old-fashioned wicker rocking chairs on the long porch of the Red Lion Inn in Stockbridge, Massachusetts. To my as-

1. According to the inconclusive account of the first meeting of the group, it was almost certainly held in May 1928. The minutes of subsequent meetings are now in the archives of the Schlesinger Library at Radcliffe. I regret that poor health has made it impossible for me to check names in these records.

tonishment, these impressive ladies were quite content to rock, not interested in the walks and hikes suggested and undertaken by the younger fry, as well as some of the other older members. From Vassar, Violet Barbour and Louise Fargo Brown came, and since both had written in my own field of seventeenth-century England it was stimulating to talk with them. Vera Brown Holmes from Smith is one whom I remember fondly, for her warmth and genuine interest in everyone made each meeting she attended a better one. Viola Barnes[2] from Mt. Holyoke, whom I already knew, was an organizer and leader of our outdoor ventures, particularly the trek through the Icy Glen. Vi was always an active participant in our evening discussions of history and of women's problems in the profession. In later years Helen Taft Manning from Bryn Mawr was a valuable addition to the group. Other older members of the group were Louise Loomis and Frances Relf from Wells (two of the founders), Beatrice Reynolds from Connecticut College, the able secretary of the association for many years, Elsie Gulley from Wheaton, Edith Farnham and Amy Gilbert from Elmira, and a Miss Young from (I think) Hunter. Once or twice Dorothy Stimpson from Gou-

2. Vera and Viola were both over ninety years old when they died recently: they were, I believe, the last of the older historians in the association.

cher, a specialist in the history of science, also came.

Of course it was good to see so many of those who were my contemporaries, given a few years up or down. From Vassar, Mildred Campbell and Evalyn Clark, Jean Wilson from Smith, Elizabeth Kimball from Wells or Mt. Holyoke, Jane Ruby from Wheaton, and Gerda Richards Crosby and Lois Merk from Radcliffe. Although each was already a friend as a result of other contacts, it was good to renew both personal and professional talk with them, as we walked, climbed mountains, or enjoyed leisurely meals at Stockbridge or Egremont.

From the beginning historians from Hunter played an important part in the conference. A group from there always arrived by train (which actually ran then to Stockbridge) or by limousine from New York. Bea Hyslop, who unfortunately died in the seventies, before she could write the official history of the conference, was a live wire at the more formal evening discussions. Dorothy Fowler, Madeline Rice, and Naomi Chergin from Hunter were valuable members also. Mary Gambrell from Hunter became, because of contacts made here, one of my best friends, and I paid a tribute to her at the conference after her death. Madeline Robinton from Brooklyn was another member it was good to see there. Nancy Norton from Wheaton was for many years our fine secretary.

Until after World War Two the membership was limited to historians at colleges in New England, New York, and New Jersey, but many of us wanted it extended. As president from 1948 to 1950, without a vote at an earlier conference, I invited Caroline Robbins of Bryn Mawr and Mary Albertson of Swarthmore to join us.[3] Because everyone liked them I was forgiven, and thenceforth we invited and welcomed new members from even further afield geographically.

Speaking in 1983 as an oldster, I may say that the conference welcomed real "youngsters" in the fifties and sixties, when a number of them joined the group. I'm happy and proud that I brought several of them there for the first time—Emiliana Noether, Jessie Lutz, Sandy Cooper, Jane Mathews, Sabra Meservey, Jean Sidar, and Mollie Swartz, all of whom were at one time or another at Douglass. Mollie told me later how much it meant to her to meet and talk into the small hours with women, young and old, from other colleges about history and the problems of women in the profession. Alison Olson from Smith, whom I met and interviewed here, shortly joined the Douglass department because her husband was coming to Princeton.

3. Often they came by train to New Brunswick, and I then drove them and Ruth Emery from Douglass to the Berkshires. How we all enjoyed this beautiful spring drive north!

The two favorite meeting-places were at the Red Lion Inn in Stockbridge and the Egremont Inn in Egremont, both in the Berkshires. The manager of the Red Lion Inn favored our group with very low rates and a luncheon picnic with lobster salad at his private retreat in the neighboring woods. And why such attention to lady historians? Because he and Emily Hickman, one of the conference's founding mothers and early presidents, had become good friends during a long journey on the trans-Siberian railroad.

The professional and social were mixed at conference meetings. As we took long walks, talk shifted from history to the beauty of the spring flowers. When the distinguished English historian Helen Cam was a visiting professor at Harvard she came to several meetings. With her love of flowers, she did not notice, or ignored, the sign that none must be picked in a special flower preserve which we visited. None of us reminded her that her beautiful bouquet of flowers was stolen treasure.

On Saturday evening the annual meeting took place. After a brief transaction of the conference's business (mainly election of officers), there were no papers, but each of the members reported on her own research, its nature, progress, and problems. A reader of this essay obviously wants to know about our concern with and discussion of the status of women historians. This problem came up particularly at the Saturday evening meeting—the opportunities for women to secure a position or move to a better one, and salary differences and other discriminations. We pooled our knowledge and thoughts on these topics, at times we proposed remedies to improve the picture, but, if my memory can be trusted, I don't think that the question of women in the historical profession was as burning an issue as it has become in recent years. Of course we were concerned, but we cared more about the opportunity provided to meet and talk history with other women historians.

This opportunity was extended each time the Berkshire Association held a breakfast meeting at the December convention of the American Historical Association for all women historians wishing to talk with us.

Certainly the members of the conference were not researching or writing women's history. Their historical writings covered a wide range of topics and countries. The greatest number chose English history—why, I wonder? Authors and their books on England in the seventeenth century comprised: Frances Relf, editing with Notestein and Simpson the seven-volume *Commons Debates in 1621*; Violet Barbour, *Henry Bennett, Earl of Arlington*; Mary Keeler, *The Long Parliament*; Mildred Campbell,

The English Yeoman under Elizabeth and the early Stuarts; Carolyn Robbins, whose *Eighteenth Century Commonwealth Man* dealt also with the later seventeenth-century commonwealth men in England; myself, with *The Crisis of the Constitution*;[4] and, last but not least, Louise Fargo Brown from Vassar. In 1911, L. F. Brown's *Political Activities of the Baptists and Fifth Monarchy Men in England during the Interregnum* had received the Herbert Baxter Adams prize of the A.H.A. in European history. In later years many new books on the radicals in mid-seventeenth-century England have appeared—on the Levellers, Diggers, and Quakers —and also Christopher Hill's *The World Turned Upside Down*. Louise Brown also wrote *Freedom of the Seas*, and *Apostle of Democracy*, the life of Lucy Maynard Salmon, the only book (I believe) coming from the group in earlier years on women's history.

Several members chose to write on more modern English history: Helen Taft Manning, *British Colonial Government after the American Revolution*;

4. Most of those listed above have produced other books in seventeenth-century English history, but I have cited only the best known one by each. I have not mentioned their magazine articles or reviews. With the materials available to me only in New Brunswick, I regret that undoubtedly I have omitted some other Berkshire members and their books. I have included only such books as I could discover which were published by members up to 1970.

Judith Williams, *British Commercial Policy and Trade Expansion, 1750–1850*; Elsie Gulley, *Joseph Chamberlain and English Social Politics*; and Alison Olson, *Anglo-American Politics, 1660–1775*. Again those members researching and writing in the medieval period mostly chose English history: Elizabeth Kimball continued Bertha Putnam's investigations of the justices of the peace, editing more of those important records, such as *Records of some Sessions of the Peace in Lincolnshire, 1381–1396*. Mary Albertson wrote *London Merchants and their Landed Property during the Reigns of the Yorkists*; Leona Gabel, *Benefit of Clergy in England in the later Middle Ages*; Anna Campbell, *The Black Death and Men of Learning*; and Norma Adams, *Select Canterbury Cases, c. 1200–1301*. Catherine Sims from Atlanta edited *Expedicio billarium antiquetus*.

Others published books in American history: Viola Barnes, *The Dominion of New England*; Vera Holmes, *A History of the Americas*; Mary Gambrell, *Ministerial Training in Eighteenth Century New England*; Dorothy Fowler, *John Coit Spooner, Defender of Presidents*; Emily Hickman, *The American Board of Customs Commissioners*; Madeline Robinton, *An Introduction to the Papers of the New York Prize Court, 1861–65*; Mary Dunn, *William Penn, Politics and Conscience*;

Mary Benson, *Women in Eighteenth Century America*; Madeline Rice, *American Catholic Opinion in the Slavery Controversy*; Catherine Cline, *Recruits to Labor*; Jane Mathews, *The Federal Theater 1935–39*; Ella Handen, *Neutrality Legislation and Presidential Discretion*; and Frances Childs, *French Refugee Life in the United States, 1790–1800*.

In French history our authors were: Beatrice Hyslop, with *A Guide to the General Cahiers of 1786*; Wilma Pugh, *Talleyrand in America as a Financial Promoter*; Beatrice Reynolds, *Proponents of Limited Monarchy in Sixteenth Century France*; Louise Dalby, *Léon Blum, Evolution of a Socialist*; and Nellie Hoyt, *History in the Encyclopédie*. In Italian history, Emiliana Noether wrote *Seeds of Italian Nationalism, 1700–1815*, and Blanche Cook wrote a *Bibliography on Peace Research in History*.

In Chinese history, Jessie Lutz wrote *China and the Christian Colleges*, Meribeth Cameron, *China, Japan and the Powers*, and Ying-Wan Cheng, *Postal Communication in China and its Modernization, 1860–1896*.[5]

It is commonly known that historians (both men and women) often seem to be chosen as administra-

5. Again, many of the authors cited in these different fields wrote other historical works, and I have included only those books that I could discover which were published by members up to 1970.

tors in their universities or colleges. Mary Gambrell became the president of Hunter, Meribeth Cameron the academic dean and acting president of Mt. Holyoke, Jean Sidar was the first Douglass alumna to become a vice president of Rutgers, Evalyn Clark was the academic dean of Vassar, Jane Ruby became dean of Wheaton, Mary Keeler became dean of Hood and I was acting dean of Douglass. In July 1982 Mary Hartman became dean of Douglass.

For about forty years the Berkshire Historical Association had been a small but vital organization in the east. Two of its younger members, Mary Hartman and Lois Banner of Douglass, then suggested that this group of women historians take a big leap into the future and sponsor a conference focusing on the growing importance of women's history, to which a large number of scholars working in that field should be invited to come and present papers on that subject. As a result of Mary's and Lois' inspired idea and careful planning, the first such conference was held at Douglass in 1973, and subsequent meetings every two or three years at Radcliffe, Bryn Mawr, Mt. Holyoke, Vassar, and in June 1984 at Smith. How fortunate it was that the original Berkshire Historical Association was there to sponsor this great extension of its longtime concern with women historians! The original association lives on as part of the larger association, and the smaller group, made up of older and younger women historians in the northeast, meets once a year in the spring, often still in the Berkshires. The annual meeting of the smaller group is more structured than in past years, but much walking and informal talking take place, just as in the past.

England–1926, 1932
and Later

IN THE AUTUMN of 1926, with a Radcliffe Travelling fellowship of $1200 making it just possible to continue the research necessary for my dissertation, I set sail for England. As the small ocean liner sailed by the nearby Irish coast and then, bound for Liverpool, entered the Irish Sea, affording glimpses of England and Wales, it was hard to believe that I was actually nearing the "promised land." Even when another Radcliffe graduate student and I settled in our third-floor apartment on Bloomsbury Street and discovered that the bathtub with its geyser for hot water occupied most of the kitchen, and that all heat for the apartment must be provided by pennies inserted in the gas fireplace, we were not indignant but amused by "quaint English ways."

Near the apartment was the British Museum, whose North Library contained the Thomason Tracts, that marvelous collection of pamphlets and newspapers which had poured from the English press between 1640 and 1660. What a debt all future historians owed to George Thomason, who had had the foresight to buy these tracts as they appeared, often daily! The wealth of material they contain on political, constitutional, military, social, and religious questions—the range of thought from conservative to radical—still draws numerous scholars to search their riches. (They are now being microfilmed.)

Close at hand, near the Museum, was the Institute of Historical Research, to which English and American professors and graduate students often went in the late afternoon for a cup of tea before continuing their work in the reference books and other secondary sources in the Institute's library. In 1926/7 Professor Alfred F. Pollard was giving his renowned weekly seminar for graduate students working in the sixteenth and seventeenth centuries, in which I enrolled. Here Professor Pollard gave advice, answered questions, and suggested research approaches to about a dozen students working on many different projects. Two of Pollard's colleagues or assistants, Eliza Davis and Charles H. Williams, were present also. Miss Davis, a tireless researcher and expert on London history, seemed to me, even before our women's lib attitudes, too subservient to Professor Pollard, whereas I soon came to respect and admire the contributions of the young C. H. Williams.

My first scholarly sojourn in England began with high hopes but, alas, lasted only from October 1926 to mid March 1927. A wrong prescription for glasses that I had been given in America caused my eyes to blur and tire too quickly as I read those musty seventeenth-century tracts. As fog settled down in London and damp chilly weather prevailed indoors as well as outdoors, my general health deteriorated. Although I continued to work as much as possible, I did not have the money to seek more comfortable living or adequate medical help. Consequently, it did not seem fair or honest to continue to live on my fellowship money when the results of my work were so meager. With a sad heart I came home to my parents in America and returned the remainder of the fellowship money to Radcliffe. In June 1931, when I went to England once more, Professors Neilson and Putnam of Mt. Holyoke helped to persuade Radcliffe to let me have this amount back again.

During 1927/8, while living at home, my good health slowly came back, as did the desire to return to England, but first I had to work, and did for three years at the New Jersey College for Women. Frustrating as this setback in my academic plans seemed at the time, in retrospect it probably was fortunate that I came to N.J.C. before the depression made it so difficult, particularly for women, to secure a teaching position in college.

In June 1931 I set sail for England again, knowing I could return to N.J.C., for Dean Douglass had happily granted me, though only an instructor, a leave of absence, for which I sincerely thank her. In London I delved again into the Thomason Tracts, spent a month working in the Bodleian Library in Oxford, wrote the thesis, and in August 1932 sent it to Professor McIlwain. Earlier that year I had sent him a thirty-page outline of my proposed thesis, but he never replied to the letter. Nevertheless, he accepted the final thesis without any changes or revisions. Part of it was published in a festschrift for him in 1936 when he became the president of the American Historical Association.

Again my thanks go to the British Museum (and particularly its North Library) and to the Institute of Historical Research for their assistance and kindness to an American woman scholar. The officials at the library of Lincoln's Inn,[1] however, seemed to have their doubts about this American woman who wished to look at certain of their legal manuscripts.

1. Lincoln's Inn was one of the "Inns of Court," where ever since the Middle Ages would-be lawyers had lived and worked as apprentices to the lawyers associated with the particular Inn.

Though properly introduced by a letter from the Institute, I was seated with the desired manuscripts at a table between two librarians. Other researchers that day, mostly men from India, were working unguarded at smaller tables around the large room. Apparently the only woman scholar in the room had to be carefully watched. Why? I can only guess that the male librarians in that masculine sanctuary wondered why a woman should be interested in manuscripts, and in particular in those dealing with legal material —hardly a woman's field.

The year spent in London in 1931/2 was entirely different from my unhappy experience there four years earlier. New and lasting friends were made, both English and American, and I came to know and love London and other parts of the British Isles. My cabin-mate on the ship to London chanced to be Christie Booth, an English lady teaching in Toronto, who was returning to England for her vacation. We bought a secondhand car for £20, in which we drove to visit friends of hers south of Edinburgh. To see the Yorkshire moors, York and Durham cathedrals, the Cheviot hills, and Edinburgh was an experience I'll never forget.

When I returned to London to work, Raymond (later Sir Raymond) Unwin[2] and his wife, relatives of Chris to whom she had introduced me, often took me under their wing, inviting me to their home on the edge of Hampstead Heath, on which we took a brisk walk before Sunday supper. Through them I had the opportunity to participate in the 1931 election in a town near London: using our car (still holding together), I picked up Labourites and took them to the polls. It was Mrs. Unwin who invited me to attend a formal birthday party arranged by Indian ladies for Mahatma Gandhi, who was at that time attending the Commonwealth Conference in London. Clad in his habitual loincloth and shawl, he walked down the aisle to the platform, where the Indian ladies, wrapped in their beautiful many-colored saris, greeted him, almost worshipping him.

At the inexpensive boarding-house near the Museum where I lived, there was another American, Ruth Collins, who was working on her Bryn Mawr dissertation. She and her friend, Katherine Garvin (the daughter of J. Garvin, the newspaper editor),[3] Margaret McGregor, on leave from Smith, and I carried on numerous heated discussions of matters political, literary, and religious in Katherine's apartment. Occasionally on a weekend we drove out of London in my antique car to enjoy the nearby coun-

2. In later years, when Sir Raymond was a visiting lecturer on architecture at Columbia, he spoke to an interested group at N.J.C.

3. Katherine edited the *Great Tudors* later.

tryside. During the winter Angus and Kitty Dun chose the same boarding-house for their London home while he was carrying on research on the Elizabethan Anglican church. How fortunate Ruth and I were, for each of us became their lifelong friends! Although Angus had a wooden leg, I remember many delightful bicycle rides with the Duns when in May 1932 the four of us worked at the Bodleian. In later years I attended Angus' consecration as Bishop of Washington and kept in touch with him and Kitty when I was in southern New Hampshire and they in northern Massachusetts. I last saw him in 1972, when they came to lunch in my lakeside Spofford cottage. "Tell us," he asked, "how do you make such a good martini?" As all the friends of this deeply spiritual, delightful, and wise man know, Angus was a "man for all seasons."

Yes, that year spent in London, 1931/2, was perhaps the most interesting and satisfying of my life. It was then that I came to know London—its bookstores and clothes-shops, its cathedrals and churches, its pubs, and its byways. One of my most treasured books is Henry Smith's sermons, published in 1610, discovered when I climbed a ladder to look over the books on the top shelf of a bookstore. At that time, old sermons were ignored by historians, and also by the proprietor of that store. How much is this book? I "innocently" asked. When told six pence, it quickly became mine, for I knew that in the early seventeenth century probably more copies of the sermons of this popular Elizabethan preacher were sold than of Shakespeare's plays.

Why do not standard tours of London today introduce Americans to the fascinating and historic Inns of Court, which are a joy to walk through? Or to the Temple Church, where at a Sunday service they pray that present and future lawyers from the Inn may continue to serve their fellow men and their nation?

In the summer of 1931 a large international academic conference was held at the University of London, and I, since I was the only member of the Rutgers faculty there, was asked, though still an instructor, to be its delegate. How surprised I and the delegates from English universities were to find me marching in the academic procession ahead of the delegates from all the British universities except Oxford, Cambridge, and St. Andrews! After all, Rutgers was founded in 1766. As one of the special events of the conference, we enjoyed tea on the terrace of the House of Commons, overlooking the Thames. The invitation to *Margaret* Judson to attend the evening reception given by His Majesty's Government stated that "tails and black tie" should be worn.

Still fond of sports, I played tennis on the courts

at Lincoln's Inn and on a winter's evening often skated on an indoor rink. In February I went to Switzerland, where I skied (very badly) in Wengen and basked in the beauty of the snowy mountains. The vacation ended with a trip to Geneva, where the 1932 disarmament conference was in session. Through the kindness of Mary Woolley, president of Mt. Holyoke and an American delegate to the conference, I received a ticket to attend a session. How fervently I hoped that this conference would bring about a world where wars would be no more!

After receiving a Ph.D. in January 1933 and the experience of teaching several different courses at N.J.C., I wished to embark on further research in seventeenth-century English history. In the summers of 1936 and 1938 I therefore returned to England.

During each of those years I also visited Germany, for the thirties were the years when Hitler came to power. As the boat train on which in 1936 I had embarked alone was approaching the border of Germany in that eerie hour just before daybreak, I wondered if I had been foolish to undertake this journey. Fearful that the liberal English periodicals (the *New Statesman* was one) with me might be noticed by Nazi officials, I tried to hide them. When the train stopped at the first German station, we were greeted by Nazi flags displayed over the whole platform and Nazi soldiers goosestepping and saluting. When, however, I joined the tour arranged in London, my fears evaporated. Never again did we see such a display of Nazi might. In fact in one town we visited, when I lost my hat in the village square, it was picked up by a Nazi soldier and returned to me with a low bow. After breakfast at a hotel on the northern shore of Lake Constance, I took a walk along a lovely wooded path near the lake, and suddenly came upon a large sign fastened to a tree which read "Verboten." Stopping short and returning to the hotel, I never knew what lay in that forbidden territory.

In June 1938 an American friend, her father and I, bound for Sweden and Finland, had a day's train journey across Germany. In our compartment sat a much-decorated Nazi official who said he was going to hunt wolves. I felt sorry for the wolves. I decided to try to discuss Hitler's future plans with this official. I knew that Austria had already been taken over by Hitler, and that his next move might be to take over the Sudeten region of Czechoslovakia, many of whose inhabitants were Germans. Mustering up my courage and my halting inadequate German, I inquired about Hitler's intentions concerning the Sudetens. They are next, he replied. But, said I, won't that mean a European war? "We have our ways," he said—and they did, for no war broke out for over a year.

After the European trip, I returned in July to London to work. Late in September came the Munich crisis. When Chamberlain returned to London, the French ministers met with the British. At about ten o'clock in the evening I went to join the crowds near 10 Downing Street, which was ablaze with lights from top to bottom, making me aware that I was close to a momentous turning-point in history. Chamberlain had proclaimed that his talks with Hitler had been successful and that he had brought back "peace in our time." My memory is that the huge crowds that night were deliriously happy that Chamberlain had saved England from war. No protesting Churchill dampened their enthusiasm. When the full story of the Munich crisis is written objectively, it will certainly include the reasons for the pacific attitudes of the English people in the thirties, and also the fact that Chamberlain's actions in September 1938 gave England a year in which to build the aircraft and train the pilots which defeated the German air attack on England in the summer of 1940.

It is fortunate that I did begin considerable basic research in England before the war.

Research: as a Historian

At N.J.C. (in the thirties) there was none of that feeling or pressure that one must "publish or perish" which later came to prevail. I was impressed, however, as mentioned earlier, by the informal reports of their own continuing research from the older women historians at the Berkshire Conference, by Louise F. Brown and Violet Barbour from Vassar for example. But most significant in my own desire to carry on further research was my dissatisfaction with the traditional interpretations historians gave of the constitutional background of the English civil war.

"For the past three hundred years," I wrote in the preface to my *Crisis of the Constitution*, "distinguished historians have told and retold the story of England's constitutional and political struggle in the seventeenth century. Nevertheless, the student and teacher of English history in this period still comes upon certain questions which send him to the sources to try to discover his own answers. Fortunately for his investigations, there exist not only the law reports and treatises, state and family papers, and printed tracts and sermons of the period, but also the newly available parliamentary diaries edited in recent years by Wallace Notestein, Hartley Simpson, Frances Relf, David Willson, and Willson Coates. The wealth of ideas revealed in these diaries convinced me that it was time for a reevaluation and interpretation of English constitutional and political thought in the first half of the seventeenth century."

In the thirties there was not only no pressure to publish at Douglass—there was no policy of leaves of absence and no Rutgers Research Council to encourage and finance research and publication. In 1938/9, however, I received the Bardwell Memorial Fellowship from Mt. Holyoke, which, with my own savings, made it possible for me to spend a year in research. After the decision had been made to go ahead on scanty funds, out of the blue came a check for $1000 from the Rutgers President, Robert Clothier, who apparently had learned of this woman at N.J.C. embarking on further research. I hope he knew how much this unexpected money did to make my year not only more profitable, but pleasant. Part of my time was spent in England, part at Harvard, several months working in the office of Professor Notestein at Yale—who kindly let me (not one of his former students) use the unedited typescript diaries of the 1624, 1625/6, and 1628 Parliaments kept by members of the Commons. I also spent months at the Huntington Library in California.

My main objective was to discover the light that primary sources might throw on the constitutional and political ideas held from 1603 to 1642. Entering upon the task with no preconceived ideas or a research model, for months I let the sources speak to me. In two of the best reviews of *The Crisis of the Constitution* each of the writers emphasized the variety of primary sources I had investigated.

After months of living with the sources I came to realize that vocal Englishmen, whether members of the Commons or of the king's council, lawyers or preachers, held a common core of constitutional and political ideas. The first three chapters of the book set forth and analyzed the ideas they held in common. Some scholars, I believe, consider these chapters the best in the book. In any case, they certainly constitute a necessary and integral part of it.

Any scholar well knows how long days, weeks, and even months of research yield too little of the information one is seeking. In retrospect, however, certain moments of excitement still come to mind. There was no indication in the Calendar of State Papers Domestic that the Public Record Office manuscript of the Petition of Right would have scribbled on the margin Archbishop Laud's comments upon it.[1] Or that in the Harvard Law Library I would find Attorney General Heath's scribbled footnote in his copy of Staunford's Plees del Coron[2] or his reaction to the 1641 statute abolishing the Star Chamber and restricting the power of the Privy Council. To come upon, in 1939 in the largely unclassified manuscripts of the Huntington Library in California, the comments of the members of the House of Lords on the final draft of the Petition of Right[3] made this researcher feel she was actually present when, over three centuries ago, the debates were taking place.

Almost every day when I was working in Professor Notestein's office on the unpublished manuscripts of the Commons in '24, '25/6, and '28, some idea or phrase uttered by a member stood out. In 1625 Robert Phelps said, "We are the last monarchy in Christendom that retain our own original rights and constitutions."[4] It seemed too good to be true that Robert Filmer's arguments in favor of taking the Engagement were actually there in manuscripts at the Bodleian. Time and time again the countless

1. State Papers Domestic 16/96:31.
2. Treasure Room, Harvard Law School Library.
3. Ellesmere MSS., nos. 7785, 7786, 7787, 7788.
4. Commons Debates in 1625. This remark from my book has been quoted several times by later historians.

Thomason Tracts worked over in the North Library would suggest a new approach or idea to be further investigated. Let me thank again the courteous help given me by the librarians of the North Library. In 1952, when I first returned after the war, a librarian quietly and casually remarked, "Good to see you here again, Miss Judson."

The first review of *The Crisis of the Constitution* appeared in an issue of the *Saturday Review of Literature* devoted to the books of university presses, and it was a devastating one. The book, according to that reviewer, was a jumble of miscellaneous sources, tossed together with no rhyme or reason. My guess is that the magazine decided that one of the books reviewed should be by a woman, and someone with no knowledge or interest in history was delegated to write the review. Shaken as naturally I was by that review, I knew the book wasn't that bad, but I could hardly believe it when the excellent reviews of the book by historians and political scientists appeared. Here are some excerpts from them.

The significance of Professor Judson's work . . . derives both from the range of sources she has used and from the breadth and penetration of her analysis. . . . Noting the dearth of profound, realistic, or logical speculation on politics before the great outpouring of 1642 to 1660, Miss Judson analyzes the common core of understanding among Englishmen while the rift in their society was developing. The civil war may have been inevitable, but Miss Judson reveals, for the reluctant fighters, it was unnatural. . . . She wastes no time in disparaging the work of other historians but demonstrates her conclusions with convincing force. She has made hers an indispensable book for students of the great controversy among Englishmen. . . . In an illuminating book she has combined detachment with a feeling for ideas that matter.[5]

How satisfying it is, in an age much given to serving up hasty puddings, to come upon an author that has so thoroughly assimilated her materials. . . . Her story is developed with skill and critical acumen.[6]

This is a scholarly and stimulating book which students of constitutional history will be using for a long time. . . . She has described admirably the making of the political mind in the first half of the century.[7]

The author of this last review also wrote to me personally, "It is the kind of study which has been needed for a long time and in your hands it has been written with great skill and rare judgment."[8]

5. Willson H. Coates, *American Historical Review*, July 1950, pp. 887–8.

6. Mildred Campbell, *The Annals*, July 1950, p. 187.

7. Hartley Simpson, *Political Science Quarterly*, March 1950, p. 468.

8. Letter to me from Hartley Simpson (Yale), January 1, 1950.

Since *The Crisis of the Constitution* was published in 1949, it has been reprinted three times, in 1964, 1971, and 1976, by Farrar, Straus & Giroux. It is still in print, and in January 1983 I received a royalty of $119 from its sales in 1982.

In the last few years it has received favorable comments from eminent British historians. In reviewing another book[9] in the *Times Literary Supplement*, November 3, 1978, Conrad Russell wrote: "This book is a brave attempt to tackle a number of difficult questions, but it will not offer a serious challenge to the work of Margaret Judson. She has recently been severely criticized for using Whiggish terminology, but for the sheer factual accuracy with which she reported what she read, she deserves her reputation as the Gardiner of political ideas."[10] In 1981 Christopher Hill wrote: "Professor Judson thirty years ago produced a powerful case for seeing consistent policies in the House of Commons in defence of property against the prerogative, throughout the first four decades [of the seventeenth century] . . . a defence which was sometimes aggres-

9. Eccleshall, Robert, *Order and Reason in Politics: Theories of Absolute and Limited Monarchy in Early Modern England*, Oxford University Press, 1978.

10. S. R. Gardiner's ten volumes on the history of England from 1603 to 1642 are regarded still as the best factual account of those years.

sive, elevating the Commonwealth above the king."[11]

The last footnote I have come upon citing *The Crisis of the Constitution* for one of the author's arguments appeared in the *Historical Journal* of December 1982.

No review, however, pleased me more than the reply I received from Charles McIlwain in 1954 when I had asked him to write the Guggenheim Foundation concerning me. "In the future," he wrote, "please take it for granted that I am only too glad to write in support of any application of yours of this kind, and don't wait to ask me. I would not do this for anyone except a scholar of whose work I am very proud."

During many trips to England over the years, I was privileged to become acquainted with a number of seventeenth-century British historians. A talk over lunch with Veronica (now Dame Veronica) Wedgwood[12] led us back into the court and pageantry of Charles I, "the happiest monarch," to Strafford, his staunch supporter, and Pym, Vane the Younger, St. John, and others who slowly and reluctantly opposed Charles' maneuvers and them-

---

11. "Parliament and People in 17th-century England," in *Past and Present: A Journal of Historical Studies*, August 1981, p. 108.

12. Author of *The King's Peace*, etc.

selves pursued policies ultimately resulting in the civil war. Fortunately for me, Veronica spent two years at the Institute for Advanced Study in nearby Princeton. Several times she graciously agreed to speak to a joint session of my undergraduate and graduate Tudor-Stuart classes: both my students and a number of faculty also present were delighted by her lectures and charm. When *The Crisis of the Constitution* appeared, it was she who first called it to the attention of scholars in England. Marjorie Blatcher and her husband Tim Bindoff[13] were long-time friends, whom it was always good to see and talk with in London or in their suburban home. When I read, first of Marjorie's death, and more recently of Tim's, it was hard to believe that never again would London be the same for me. It was they and Veronica who introduced me at lunch or dinner to the inner sanctity of an English club. Helen Cam,[14] whom I had come to know at the Berkshire Conference, entertained me at her country home and wrote to several Cambridge historians when she heard in 1955 that I was spending May in the Cambridge libraries. Her remark that my *Crisis of the Constitution* was "a jolly good book" warmed my heart.

13. Tim was the author of *Tudor England*, etc. Marjorie wrote several historical articles.

14. Author of *The Hundred and the Hundred Rolls*.

How fortunate I was in recent years to know Valerie Pearl![15] With her, as with Veronica Wedgwood, I engaged in many interesting discussions in both London and New Brunswick, When she came to this country to teach at Bryn Mawr for a semester, she spent a weekend in my apartment. Her lecture at Rutgers again afforded my students and others the opportunity to hear an English professor actively engaged in research on previously untouched sources speaking on London's part in the civil war. May I thank her here for the advice she generously gave when a woman with a Rutgers Ph.D., who had worked with me, sought it when she was in London?

Only very recently did I come to know Christopher Hill,[16] who taught at Rutgers from September to Christmas 1981. He most generously gave a number of lectures and led discussions for interested groups, opening up for all present a new understanding of Milton and the "World Turned Upside Down," even in the seventeenth century. Although his numerous writings and my few approached English history in the seventeenth century from different vantage points, in conversing with Christopher I always found a common ground where I

15. Author of *London and the Outbreak of the Puritan Revolution*, etc.

16. Author of *The World Turned Upside Down*, etc.

(at least) learned much. Like the English historians mentioned earlier, he too was charming, as was his wife, a historian working in women's history.

There were other English historians who, although I did not know them as well as those mentioned above, always made me welcome. When in London I often dropped into Professor John Neale's[17] seminar, and he always encouraged me to participate in the discussion. The month of May 1955, as I have said, was spent in Cambridge, carrying on research in the different college libraries (primarily St. John's). When Professor Peter Laslett[18] heard that I was there, he arranged a luncheon to introduce me to other Cambridge historians, including the formidable Geoffrey Elton,[19] whom I met for the first time. Laslett also entertained me at his home.

All the English historians whom I came to know were most cordial to an American historian writing British history. The fact that I happened to be a woman did not seem to perplex or disturb them at all.

Of course I experienced some frustrations as a woman historian. In 1938, when given permission to work in the stacks of the Harvard Law Library, it was granted only if I entered by the *back* door.

17. Author of *The Elizabethan House of Commons*, etc.
18. Author of *The World We Have Lost*, etc.
19. Author of *The Tudor Revolution in Government*, etc.

Otherwise, the head librarian, obviously not desiring to have women researching in this male bastion, might see the woman and forbid further research there. At about the time my *Crisis* appeared, so did another good book,[20] dealing in part with the same problems as mine, by a man, George Mosse at the University of Iowa. Neither of us had known of the other's work, but the two books were occasionally reviewed in the same article. In every case, the reviewer said that my book was the better of the two. Within the year, however, he accepted a full professorship at the University of Wisconsin, whereas no offer of another position in history came to me.

Although, as indicated earlier, administrative positions had by now been offered me, none in history had been. Nor even after favorable reviews of the *Crisis* did I ever receive a letter inquiring whether I might be interested in leaving N.J.C. None of my contemporaries among women professors in the east, as far as I know, has ever left the women's college where first she was employed. Whether or not any of them could have moved to another college I do not know.

Many historians seemed surprised that a woman historian wrote upon constitutional and political ideas and had done research in legal sources. A pro-

20. *The Struggle for Sovereignty in England from the Reign of Queen Elizabeth to the Petition of Right.*

fessor at the University of Michigan, where I was a visiting professor in 1959, inquired if my interest in English literature had led me to turn to history, and seemed surprised when told that it was political science and political thought that had led me to investigate some of the political and constitutional ideas expressed in the seventeenth-century constitutional struggle in England.

As a Member of a University

MABEL DOUGLASS, the founder and first dean of N.J.C., presided over a largely autonomous college within Rutgers University, even going to Trenton herself to lobby for a separate Douglass budget for her "beloved girls." Nor did she remind us often, if at all, that Douglass was a college within Rutgers University. Yet in my first months here I remember walking across town to the Rutgers Library, housed then in the present Arts Museum. What a delight to find there so many more books in history than in the cramped quarters of the N.J.C. Library, which was housed then in part of Recitation Building! The Rutgers Library also contained some collections of valuable sources in English history. In addition to using this library as much as possible myself, I urged my junior-senior history majors to go there for their research papers. At first the librarian thought that only graduate students, and certainly not N.J.C. undergraduates, should use their primary source collections, but he soon relented in his policy. Across town was another library—the

Gardiner Sage Library of the Dutch Reformed Seminary. This beautiful library, containing a wide assortment of books in addition to the theological, was a joy to work in, and from the beginning welcomed and assisted my junior and senior students in their research.

When finally the University's Alexander Library was built, it was freely open to all members of the university. My recommendations for new books and primary source collections were solicited, and often the books were secured. After my retirement the Library provided a faculty study for me which has proved invaluable for my research on and publication of two short books written since 1967 and the writing of this essay.

The late forties and early fifties were the years, as Professor Schmidt has pointed out, when the university trustees and governors included buildings for the women's college in their plans for the future. In 1953, a student center on the N.J.C. campus was built—the first new building since 1928. In these same years, some members of the N.J.C. or Douglass faculty served on university committees, I, for example, sat on the Research Council, on the committee advisory to the president, on the graduate-school committee, and in 1952 on the faculty search committee for a new president.

After the war, too, it was good to come to know

better my colleagues in history across town—Ethan Ellis, Richard McCormick, Peter Charanis, Sidney Ratner, Herbert Rowan, Warren Susman, Eugene Genovese, and particularly Henry Winkler, Samuel McCulloch, and Richard Schlatter in English history. Years before the formal creation of the Federated College Plan in 1967/8, the Rutgers (then Arts and Science) College and Douglass history departments cooperated unofficially to avoid duplication in making new appointments in certain specialized fields, such as, for example, those of Peter Charanis in Byzantine history at Rutgers or of Margaret Hastings in medieval and myself in Tudor-Stuart England. Since Ardath Burks in the Rutgers political science department was a specialist on Japan, the Douglass department appointed in 1956 Jessie Lutz, the first specialist, I believe, in Chinese history in the university.

In the early fifties, Henry Winkler and other new young members of the Rutgers history department pointed out that it was ridiculous that I was not teaching graduate students, as they were at that time. May I comment on the fact that it was George Schmidt who insisted on my promotion to full professor and that it was younger men who worked to have me teach graduate students? The Douglass dean, however, concerned, like Mrs. Douglass, more with her college than with the university, believed it unwise to reduce my hours of teaching at Douglass, and it was not possible for me to teach graduate courses for several years. Although I still loved to teach (and did) a freshman survey course, the experience of giving a graduate research seminar to a few students, when I was finally allowed to do so, was equally challenging and rewarding. The first part of a semester was spent in introducing the students, most of whom knew little or nothing about England from 1580 to 1660, to some of the issues, personalities, and controversies of the period—and also to the primary sources in the Alexander Library dealing with these years. A student would give a brief report, using some primary sources, upon a topic generally suggested by me. I remember a good one upon Edwin Sandys, a colonizer and a leading member of Parliaments in James I's reign. A report upon John Preston, preacher *par excellence*, revealed to the students the importance of sermons for a study of this period. The reactions to and the repercussions of the Ship Money Case decision formed the subject of another valuable report. Each student chose to be a participant in the famous Putney debates of 1647—representing, for example, Rainborough and Wildman arguing for the soldiers, Ireton and Cromwell for the generals in the Parliamentary army. After each report members of the class questioned the speaker and commented upon his presentation, while I filled in the necessary background, facts, and interpretation of it.

Over the years many students understandably selected a topic dealing with one of the numerous radical groups in the late forties and early fifties. I hope that today some of them have discovered and read Christopher Hill's *The World Turned Upside Down.* In the latter part of the semester each student wrote a paper on the topic he had become conversant with, and read it to the seminar.[1]

Every other year I gave such a graduate seminar, alternating it with a more general graduate Tudor-Stuart course. In many ways I taught this course in the same way as I did my undergraduate course in the same period. Each student, however, gave a report to the class, and some topics were treated more fully, with greater emphasis on present-day controversies among historians and more use of primary sources. In supervising a Ph.D. thesis in sixteenth- or seventeenth-century English history, the problem always arose of finding a subject for which the Rutgers and neighboring libraries (in Princeton and New York) possessed adequate research materials, for Rutgers students could seldom go to England for their research. Increasingly, however, and par-

1. Four of the students from these seminars continued to work under my supervision on their Ph.D. dissertations.

ticularly since I retired, the English sources are being microfilmed and can be studied nearer home.

As has been brought out, the members of the Rutgers history departments and the university administration and university committees seemed to have accepted me as a helpful colleague, even though I was a woman. There are, however, several times when the fact that I was a woman "participating in a man's world" surprised or annoyed outsiders. In 1952, as a member of President Jones' faculty advisory committee, I was invited to his home for cocktails with the trustees who later, at dinner, were to consider the Finley-Heimlich case.[2] During the social hour one trustee remarked to me, "Don't tell me that you, a beautiful lady, are supporting Finley and Heimlich," obviously implying that women do not, or should not, have views (and particularly "radical ones") on the serious questions rightly handled by men.

In 1952 I was a member of the faculty search committee for a new president, and the meeting with

2. In 1952, during the McCarthy era, Simon Heimlich, an associate professor at the College of Pharmacy, and Moses Finley, an assistant professor of history at the Newark College of Arts and Sciences, had taken the Fifth Amendment of the United States Constitution and refused to answer questions asked by a Congressional committee concerning their alleged communist connections. See Richard P. McCormick, *op. cit.*, pp. 293–296, for further details.

one of the candidates was held in New York, either at the Harvard or at the University Club. The other woman in the group was Mrs. Katzenbach, a Rutgers trustee. The two women, however, had to dine alone in the room set apart for women, whereas the other members of the group had luncheon with the candidate in the main dining-room. Were they surprised and perhaps annoyed when the candidate joined the two women for quite a time? Could it be, perhaps, for that reason that they didn't choose this candidate? He, however, was my first choice, for several reasons in addition to his courtesy towards women.

One evening the Rutgers graduate faculty met with its graduate students, and the chairman talked to the students about possible future jobs, pointing out how difficult, indeed almost impossible, it was for women to secure positions in college. Some of the women in my own graduate seminar asked me to talk to them and other women graduate students about the situation, and I agreed to meet with them informally one evening. At that time I assured them that good women could secure jobs teaching history in college. They must, however, be mindful of certain types of behavior that men colleagues would hold against them. They must not ask for or take special privileges as women. If they had children, for example, they must provide in advance for someone to attend to their minor ills: only in a real emergency should they stay home to care for them.

I never felt any conflict between my continuing loyalty to Douglass and my growing loyalty to the university. Both loyalties seemed natural and both enriched my many years here.

The University of Michigan
and the Bunting Institute

F ROM FEBRUARY TO JUNE 1959 I was fortunate
to be the visiting Alice Freeman Palmer Professor of History at the University of Michigan
in Ann Arbor. Professor Carolyn Robbins of Bryn
Mawr was the first woman holding this position, in
1958, and had recommended me to be the second.
Women graduates of the university, unhappy that
there were no tenured women in the history department, had endowed the position, stipulating that the
woman should be a full professor. After Carolyn and
I had served as visiting professors, Sylvia Thorpe
was appointed as a regular professor in the department. It is natural to assume that the department,
skeptical of women professors, first wanted a "trial
run," and Carolyn and I must have answered some
of their doubts.

When I came to know members of the department, one told me that they had never questioned
my scholarship or ability to teach, but had feared

that the presence of a woman in department meetings would inhibit men from smoking or putting their feet up on chairs. When I first drove into Ann Arbor on a snowy February evening, and inquired whether I might park in the university's lot, the attendant asked if I was a new professor's wife or his secretary. When I replied that I was *the* professor, the astonished attendant did allow me to park.

Apart from these amusing incidents, I can only report that my semester at Ann Arbor was a stimulating and delightful one. The department made me welcome, and the students, both undergraduate and graduate, were a joy to teach. In general I followed the same pattern in teaching as I had done at Douglass and Rutgers. In a large undergraduate class of juniors and seniors I gave more formal lectures than at Douglass, but eventually I introduced student discussion into the class. The graduate seminar consisted of about a dozen students, several of them excellent.[1] Three of their reports on Cromwell's difficult decisions—to try and execute Charles in 1649, to dissolve the Rump Parliament in 1653, and to refuse the offer of the crown in 1657—proved to be most interesting and valuable. Teaching only two courses, the common practice now for many

1. One man in the graduate seminar followed me back to Rutgers, eventually writing his doctoral thesis under my supervision.

Rutgers professors, but not in my time, gave me the opportunity to spend much time in the library and to counsel my students. In fact, I asked Professor Wilcox, the department chairman, if there was a department task which could be assigned to me. He declined the suggestion, thanking me for the time I spent advising students in my office, and implying subtly that some professors shirked those responsibilities, which I took for granted.

Not only was my professional life at Ann Arbor a rich one, but also my personal life. Since the fourth member of a bridge group had left, the group, learning of my fondness for bridge, invited me to take his place. As a result of our bridge games I became a lifelong friend of John and Dana Spielman. John, then an instructor at Michigan, is now a professor at Haverford. John Baldwin, also an instructor there and now a professor at Hopkins, and his charming wife are friends whom I occasionally have seen in later years. At the spring picnic of the department, to their surprise, I played for a time in the softball game, and at 59 did catch one easy ball and managed to hit a slow grounder. When some members of the department learned I was a longtime Red Sox baseball fan, they took me to a Red Sox–Tigers game in Detroit.

Yes, on all counts, the semester spent at Michigan was a happy and rewarding one. It was reassuring to know that the Michigan department asked me back in 1966/7 to replace a professor in my field who was going to be on leave. Had I not stayed on for that year as acting dean at Douglass, I certainly would have been happy to be in Ann Arbor again.

I had a second interesting and rewarding experience of teaching elsewhere in 1968/9 at the Radcliffe Bunting Institute in Cambridge. Constance Smith, a political scientist whom the Douglass department and the Eagleton Institute had brought to Douglass and Rutgers in 1955, had been chosen by Mary Bunting, dean of Douglass from 1955 to 1960, to head the new institute which she, then president of Radcliffe, had conceived and established to further the opportunities for women to carry on scholarly or creative work in Cambridge. The institute also offered seminars for which graduate credit was given in the extension unit of Harvard. The one I gave, to about a dozen students, ranging from a woman of 21 to a Boston lady 80 years old, was on the period from 1640 to 1660 in England. They worked hard, and I remember best the stimulating and often heated discussions carried on around the table on the "causes" of the civil war, the Putney debates, the trial and execution of Charles, the mushrooming of radical groups in the fifties, and of course Cromwell—his religious beliefs and his social compassion along with his built-in conservatism, and his agonizing decisions. In the discussions, an intelligent black man, about forty years old, planning to return to a government position in his native African state, was perhaps the most perceptive of the class in his remarks. And yet in his seminar paper it was clear that he had not learned how to organize his knowledge and his ideas into a coherent whole.

It was possible for me to spend about two days a a week continuing research in the Houghton Library at Harvard for my book *From Tradition to Political Reality*. Just living in Cambridge again was a delight, even though two attacks of the flu interfered with some of the things I had hoped to do.

Under the wise and charming leadership of Connie and with the support of President Bunting the Institute grew and flourished. At a sandwich luncheon the members talked informally of their projects, and in addition each of them presented her own project more formally in a special forum. Before the sad and untimely death of Constance Smith, the Institute had become an important adjunct of Radcliffe and a valuable institution furthering the opportunities for talented women. After her death, it has continued to grow and to expand many women's opportunities and achievements under Presidents Bunting and Horner of Radcliffe, Dean Alice Kimball Smith, and succeeding deans of the Institute. The reports of the varied projects and achievements of the current fellows sent me by Dean Margaret McKenna reveal the expanding role of the Institute since its inception.

The Conference
on British Studies

IN 1950 A GROUP of about fifty scholars concerned with British history met in a parlor of one of New York University's small houses on Gramercy Square. Here papers were given and discussed, luncheon served, and good talk carried on. This meeting came about because previously six professors of English history had met informally in New York and decided to form a Conference on British Studies. They had sent out invitations to fellow professors and scholars within a radius of about eighty miles of New York. Harold Hulme of N.Y.U., Jack Hexter of Queens, Jean Hecht, and Ruth Emery, Samuel McCulloch and myself of Rutgers were the six responsible for starting the Conference.

From small beginnings, the Conference grew and grew. Its members now number about one thousand and are drawn from all parts of the United States and Canada. Seven regional branches now exist: New England, Middle Atlantic states, Southern,

Midwest, Rocky Mountain, Pacific Coast, and Northwest. In each of the seven branches yearly or semi-yearly meetings are held, with the mother, now called the North American Conference, meeting in turn with each of the branches. The organization sponsors and publishes the semi-yearly *Journal of British Studies*, *The Monitor and Intelligencer*, *Studies in British Culture*,[1] etc.

In the earlier days the speakers at the New York meeting were, for the most part, visiting scholars from England, whereas at more recent meetings they were mostly American. When the eminent British historian Geoffrey Elton addressed us, I remember that finally I screwed up my courage to differ with him on some point he had made in Tudor history. Wallace Notestein from Yale was a valuable and faithful attendant at our meetings for a number of years. Among the historians I met or came to know better because of our contacts at the meetings were Herman Ausubel and Bart Brebner of Columbia, Wallace McCaffrey of Harvard, and Fred Cazel and his wife from Connecticut College. May I thank Jack Hexter publicly for his frequent favorable references to *The Crisis of the Constitution*? My many women friends from the Berkshire Conference who taught British history also

1. My 1980 book *From Tradition to Political Reality* is the seventh volume in this series.

came to meetings of the C.B.S. To see each other and renew our friendships here was always one of the joys of these meetings.

Sometime in the fifties I gave a paper at the C.B.S. program held during the December meeting of the American Historical Association. In this paper I made comparisons among the representative institutions of England, France, the Netherlands, Sweden, and Spain in the sixteenth and seventeenth centuries. Why in most countries these institutions declined in importance or died out, whereas in England Parliament grew mightily in importance, was a fascinating subject to investigate.

In 1977 I planned a visit to friends in California at the time of the national C.B.S. meeting at the Claremont Colleges. My longtime friend Sam McCulloch, always a tower of strength in the Conference, had become its president, and Henry Winkler, Dick Schlatter, and I were present from Rutgers to honor him on this occasion.

The thirtieth anniversary of the Conference was marked by a special tribute paid to its founders in December 1980. During the annual meeting of the A.H.A. a cocktail party was held in the rotunda of the British Embassy in Washington. Members of the embassy wished to recognize and thank the C.B.S. for its contribution over the years in strengthening British-American ties. At this party three of the six founders of the Conference, Samuel Mc-Culloch, Jack Hexter, and myself, were present. The president of the C.B.S. read a citation for each of us and gave us each a handwrought pewter Jefferson cup. My cup, inscribed with my name and "C.B.S. 1950–1980," is among my most treasured possessions.

As Administrator

AFTER GEORGE SCHMIDT'S resignation as chairman, the Douglass history department elected me, and I tried to continue the policies George had followed in maintaining the excellent reputation of the department. In new appointments and in later considerations for tenure both scholarship and teaching were our main criteria. Thus one productive scholar who for several years proved to be a poor undergraduate teacher was not granted tenure, but fortunately was able to go to another university where he could work with graduate students.

Not following the general policy in the Arts and Science history department, we decided to appoint a few highly qualified part-time women. When Alison Olson's husband came to Princeton, Alison joined the Douglass history department, and later Jane Mathews, employed at the nearby Educational Testing Bureau, became a part-time member also. Both proved to be excellent teachers and scholars, whom we hated to lose when their husbands left this area. And each actually devoted more than half her time to her work here, for, as they became known and admired by their students, they were asked to participate in general college affairs and occasionally speak at them. After Alison had to leave Douglass, the Rutgers College history department offered her a full-time position there—one of the first, if not the very first, offered to a woman. It is important, it seems to me, that good women should have more opportunities to hold part-time positions, not only in a college, but in other areas. It would be unwise, however, to include too many in one academic department.

I hope and believe that in department meetings I encouraged all members, women and men, full- and part-time, to participate as equals in our discussions, as earlier I had been encouraged to do. Last year, a man, now a professor, thanked me for this attitude of mine during his early years here.

All appointments and major decisions in political science were made with the full concurrence of the professors in that area. To work with Neil Mc-Donald, the senior professor in political science, was a pleasure, for we could happily reach agreement on the current issue or problem. Neil and James Rosenau wanted to secure a woman political scientist, but women in that field are admittedly harder to discover than women historians. When I took over the task and found Connie Smith, Neil and Jim were happy to have her join our department. In the few years she stayed with us, before President Bunting took her to be head of the new Radcliffe Institute, Connie quickly came to be a most valuable and beloved member of the department and college.

Although I sincerely believe that the professors in a women's college should be both men and women, I am happy that our department was composed of women as well qualified and successful as the men. When, however, I wrote in the early sixties to the chairman of the Columbia history department, asking if he would recommend a person to teach American post–Civil War history at Douglass, he replied in several paragraphs that unfortunately he had no one to suggest, and only a last sentence in his letter, almost an afterthought, reads, "Would you possibly consider a woman?"

When Alison Olson and Jane Mathews heard that I was writing this essay they asked me to let them say how much they appreciated working in the Douglass department.

"When you were Chairman of the History Department," Alison wrote, "it was more like a family than an impersonal group of professional colleagues. You gave us each love and concern, pride in our own work, respect for the accomplishments of our colleagues, and joy in being part of the group. It was you who made possible all our happy memories of that time."

Jane Mathews wrote:

Mentor, sisterhood—these words were not part of our vocabulary in 1964, but Margaret Judson gave them meaning. As a young A.B.D. and a Princeton faculty wife, I met Margaret Judson when I came to Douglass College initially on a one-year appointment. I arrived with a burning need to teach and to be taken seriously as a scholar and an equal measure of confusion and in- ner doubts as to whether women really could do those things, especially with families. Margaret Judson broke through differences of generation and of life-style to as- sure us that we could.

As former chair of the Department of History and later as Acting Dean of Douglass College, Margaret shared herself and her professional life in ways that made clear female scholars could excell and that they could be at the center, not the periphery, of a depart- ment, college, and university. As a mentor eager to socialize us in the intricacies of academic life, she must have queried us about progress on dissertations or when manuscripts would be published. But all I really recall is the unwavering expectation that we would accom- plish both.

In the spring of 1966 Ruth Adams resigned as dean to become president of Wellesley. Also in the spring the history and political science departments had given me a delightful retirement party, where colleagues, friends, and past students (both women and men) gathered to wish me well in the years of "leisure" ahead. The actual date of my retirement was June 30—but early that month came a telephone call from President Gross asking if I would serve as acting dean of Douglass for the coming year. I was surprised and doubtful as to the answer, but after a week's consideration of the offer it was yes. I am truly glad that it was.

And why was I given this opportunity and challenge? Some Douglass faculty had suggested, so I was later told, that as a longtime member of the faculty I would be their choice for acting dean. Perhaps they feared that a male administrator from Rutgers would serve in that capacity and might not sufficiently consider the special interests of Douglass in the year ahead. And although never told, I'm quite sure that the fact I'd been increasingly involved in university affairs—committees, teaching graduate students, etc.—was a major factor in President Gross' decision to ask me to serve.

The college opened in September 1966, two centuries after the founding of Rutgers. In my "inaugural" address I pointed out to the incoming freshmen that they entered a college with a rich and long heritage, reaching back, as a college within Rutgers University, two hundred years, and, as an institution of higher learning in the western world, over seven centuries. Important as a college is, in "providing the machinery and means for your education," I told the freshmen, "in the last analysis you educate yourself." "The quantity of facts and ideas you will acquire is not as important as their quality." "There is no course at Douglass, Rutgers—or any other college I know of—labeled 'The Quality of Your Ideas,' open only to seniors. . . . By searching questions the quality of your ideas deepens as your interests widen and your understanding grows. . . . Don't be scared of the unknown. Welcome it. To be aware that there are not certain answers to all questions is the beginning of wisdom."

My new task as dean was undergirded by the strong support of the faculty and the invaluable assistance of Douglass and Rutgers administrators. May I thank with all my heart Edna Newby, the associate dean, Frances Riche, the executive secretary (and soon to be assistant dean), Marjorie Trayes, dean of students, Patsy Collins Hunter, executive secretary, and Clyde McAlister, the bursar, for their expert knowledge and patience in explaining so much and advising so well an inexperienced dean! In the university administration, president Mason Gross, provost Richard Schlatter, the academic dean Albert Meder, and James Johnston were never too busy to answer my many questions and most helpful in any problem when their advice was sought.

Realizing that a new dean with fresh ideas would succeed me after a year, it seemed important that I should not initiate basic changes but do my best to leave the college in good condition for her to carry on. After 38 years of academic life and of teaching history, I had learned a great deal about human nature, vested interests, and power politics, but as dean my eyes were opened wider. Two department chairmen, for example, were frequently arguing, almost fighting, over one thing or another. After one brought his complaints to the dean, within a day, or even an hour, the other chairman would call asking for an appointment. In another department, the chairman refused to recommend the promotion to full professor of an outstanding member of the department. After sober consideration of the dilemma and with the approval of the provost, I went over the chairman's head and recommended the promotion, which went through. As a consequence, the chairman soon resigned and accepted another position. Chairmen are not always infallible in their decisions. I remember how surprised, even shocked, I was when another chairman, gentle, charming, and polite, could not understand that reduced funds for Douglass meant that each department must be cut a little, and fought like a tiger to prevent any loss for his department.

For many months I met each week with the provost and the deans of Arts and Science[1] and of Livingston[2] to discuss and agree upon a proposal for a federated college which had been initiated in the spring of 1966 by President Mason Gross. For a long time two predominantly liberal arts colleges had existed in New Brunswick: Arts and Science, located primarily on the original Rutgers College campus, and Douglass, across town about a mile away. A new third liberal arts college, Livingston, was being built across the Raritan on federal land from which in World War Two troops had embarked for Europe and which had since been given to Rutgers. To formalize into a federated system within the university these widely separated liberal arts colleges was the objective the committee worked long and hard to achieve. When our work was completed, leaving some technical problems unsolved (such as a simplified registration procedure for courses taken in the different colleges),[3] my responsibility was to explain the plan to the Douglass faculty and

1. Renamed Rutgers College during our discussions.
2. This group was joined in December (or January) by the deans of Cook and of Engineering. I do not know why University College was not included.
3. As far as I know, this technical task was never carried out.

students and urge their support for it. In 1980, when the Reorganization Plan for the university, which took the place of the Federated Plan, was adopted, many faculty and students of Douglass, who opposed the new plan, rested their case on the merits of the Federated Plan. In 1967, however, a number of faculty and students had seriously questioned and some opposed the Federated Plan. Perhaps my most difficult task that year was to conduct the Douglass faculty meetings where the Federated Plan was hotly debated. I remember that at a student meeting held to discuss the plan one student asked me, "How long has Douglass been a part of Rutgers University?"

As I was preparing to wind up the year as acting dean, there came in June the important but difficult task of recommending raises of $3000 to $5000 for full professors. After much thought and consultation, particularly with associate dean Edna Newby, I made the specific recommendations to the university administration. These took account of the length of a professor's service, his excellence, and the higher salaries which in recent years new professors had received. As far as I know, my recommendations were accepted, and the amount received by each full professor never questioned.[4]

4. I naturally regretted that these substantial salary raises, long overdue, came too late to affect me.

In the sixties with Dean Ruth Adams, President Mason
Gross, and Dorothy Quackenbass Cost

Acting Dean

In one area (and undoubtedly more) I failed miserably as an administrator. When *Caelian* (the Douglass student paper) called, asking for an immediate opinion on a current or controversial issue, it was difficult to give them a thoughtful reply. More frustrating were telephone calls from the New Brunswick *Home News* waking me up at one in the morning, asking for a quick opinion on this or that issue.

Most people have thought that the year in which I was acting dean must have been the "busiest" of my life. It most certainly was not, partly because of the help given me. In addition to the invaluable assistance of those at Douglass and Rutgers mentioned earlier, to have a competent secretary handling telephone calls, appointments, records, etc., is invaluable for any administrator. For the many years when I taught twelve hours (including three different courses) and served on Douglass and university committees, I was much "busier."

Yes, I was glad that my last year at Douglass afforded me an interesting challenge and experience. I hope that the college was left in good condition for the new dean to carry on. And also prepared to move ahead with the "courage and a spirit of adventure—to experiment with new curricula and new approaches to learning—to introduce new areas of knowledge—to work out new ways for more students to work independently."[5] George Schmidt, in his *Douglass College: A History*, wrote of me, "Hers was not a caretaker administration, and this was fortunate," citing in particular my efforts "to make the faculty, particularly its many new members, more concerned with the college as a whole."[6]

At the last faculty meeting, I was surprised and touched by the following tribute paid me:

Dear Margaret:

The members of the faculty and administration of Douglass College wish to express to you our very deep appreciation of the great service you have rendered, during this year of transition, as our Acting Dean. We have thought that as a concrete means of extending our heart-felt thanks to you, we would provide a method by which your name and your special interests will be perpetually woven into the life of the College. We have therefore raised $930 to establish an annual prize for students, which will be administered by the Department of History and will be known as the Margaret Atwood Judson Prize in History. With every recurring spring the College will thus be reminded of you and your devoted contributions to our life as scholar, teacher, and administrator.

Elizabeth Boyd
Robert Walter
Clyde McAlister

5. Article in the New Brunswick *Home News*, June 2, 1967.
6. P. 262.

The university provost wrote me the following letter:

Dear Margaret:

Now that the year has come to an end I want to write you formally to say how very much I appreciate the work you did for Douglass and the University during the past year. No one could have filled the post with the distinction and sagacity which you brought to it. I think you managed magnificently to do the difficult job of representing Douglass honestly and fairly and, at the same time, acting like a member of the full University community. I appreciate all you did very much indeed!

Sincerely,
Richard Schlatter

As Educator

THERE IS NO magic formula or curriculum, required or elective course, which will guarantee that a student, even a good one, will upon graduation be started on the way towards becoming a truly educated person. Colleges and universities, committees and individuals, have searched for over a century to find and set up a regime which will at least produce a graduate who, having been exposed to it for four years, will possess some of the knowledge, attitudes, and values which are the hallmark of an educated person.

After thirty-eight years of teaching undergraduates and considerable experience on college and university committees, as department chairman and acting dean, I have become more and more aware of and concerned with this search. Here are a few suggestions which should, in my opinion, be integrated into any plan worked out in future years.

During those four years a student should be exposed to or have contact with *greatness* and so have a chance to come to respect and value it. Let him, for example, read in its entirety Plato's *Republic* (not just excerpts from it) and come to understand that Plato is dealing with a universal problem in human society—how to produce rulers who put public concerns above private interests. Plato's *Republic*, as well as others of his works, is "for all seasons," not (as one student remarked) really pretty good for someone writing it over two thousand years ago. Again, take Burke's *Reflections on the French Revolution*. Having assigned that essay in the early forties to a bright student, knowing that she was an intellectual communist, before making any comments of my own, I asked her what she thought of it. "The best presentation and argument for conservatism I have ever read," she replied. She recognized greatness, even though completely repudiating Burke's philosophy. Thirty years later, when I met her at reunion time and she said "I'm sure you don't remember me," I hastened to assure her that I certainly did and reminded her of her comment upon Burke. When I asked a professor of English which of Shakespeare's plays she loved most to teach, year after year, understandably they were *Hamlet* and *Lear*.

In art—illuminating and important as its history is—shouldn't a student have, for example, the opportunity to study in depth a great medieval cathedral, such as Chartres or Amiens? The amazing structural technique by which flying buttresses enabled the curved arches to reach higher and higher towards heaven, thus achieving the creation in stone of Thomas Aquinas' *Summa Theologica*; and the work of medieval builders and artisans who often journeyed far for their work; and that of the carvers who wrought in stone the great biblical heroes for all—the humble and mighty—to behold; and the matchless colors and mosaic of the windows through which the sun filters in, to give the interior its subdued and mystic beauty.

I was a "late bloomer" in my love of art, which deepened with every visit to an American or European gallery. One experience stands out as the most overwhelming, perhaps even mystical. No, it was not in the Sistine Chapel, nor the Louvre, but in the Church of Santo Tomé in Toledo. Here a single painting, the "Burial of Count Orgaz," done by El Greco in 1586, whose greatness I'm not competent to explain, held me spellbound after the group of which I was a part had long since left the chapel.

It has certainly been possible for Rutgers students over the years to hear great music—whether it be the Boston Symphony under Kousevitsky, or the Philadelphia under Ormandy, or the beautifully trained Rutgers Chorus singing with the Philadelphia Orchestra in New Brunswick or New York. Many members of the Douglass and Rutgers departments and the Musica Sacra often give delightful concerts which are free for all members of the university and community.

Whether or not a student majors in science, I hope that he or she may have the experience of grasping the aesthetic beauty of a mathematical or chemical formula. What opportunities are opening up for a physics or biology or psychology major to study the wonders of recent developments in these fields? Man's investigation of the unknown, his search for the truth, has a long history, and, let us hope, a future even more rewarding, for there is so much more to be discovered. It is the *search*, as well as the past and present achievement of science, which one hopes *all* students will respect and honor. Even in fields other than science, students should come to realize that scholars are seeking and finding new facts: thus in history, for example, they are setting forth new interpretations of the past. In recent years historians have extended our knowledge of new areas, especially of women's history and African history. Yet one good lady asked me, "Why do research in history? Isn't everything known about that dead subject?"

In any subject an exceptional teacher can raise the sights of a receptive student, giving him contact with greatness. One feels sure that Mason Gross was profoundly influenced by Alfred North Whitehead.

At Mt. Holyoke, Professor Hazlett excited (dazzled?) me in mathematics, and Nellie Neilson gave new meaning and depth to history, which I had long loved. At Radcliffe, Charles McIlwain conveyed the amazing depth of his knowledge of the sources of English history and political thought, and would share his excitement over a document with his classes and even with a single student in conference. Also at Radcliffe, Charles H. Haskins opened up unknown worlds to his students.

There certainly are some good teachers who have carried on little new research since receiving their higher degrees; as well as excellent scholars who have published several learned books, and yet are generally regarded by their students as poor teachers. However, in general, I sincerely believe that a professor who either carries on research which results in publication, or, as in art or music or literature, creates as well as teaches, is the most desirable kind of college professor in a "liberal arts" college or curriculum.

A second aspiration for students, and not only those concentrating in the social sciences, is that they come to acquire some understanding of the *complexity* of many past and present problems; how, as an example, a murder in Bosnia, an Austrian province, of the heir to the Austrian throne, led step by step into World War One—a war which, in my opinion, and that of many others, few government leaders really expected or wanted (at least at that time). Had it not taken place and been so devastating and lasted so long, it can be argued that there would have been no Hitler and World War Two, no Russian Revolution and the resulting and present Communist government in the Soviet Union. For a supposedly educated person in his conversation, or for a government official in an important speech or decision, to view a complex problem in black and white terms with no shades of gray or even red in between reveals, I submit, that something has been missing or not grasped by him in his college education.

A third experience I would hope students may have is some acquaintance with and understanding of a non-western civilization, such as, for example, the Chinese, Moslem, or (even though western in some respects) the Russian. Whether it be through history, political science, sociology, philosophy, religion, art, or literature, to be cognizant of non-western achievements, ways of thinking, and values is fascinating and increasingly important for those in our western world. Such an experience helps the student also better to understand our western culture and might enable him, if he is fortunate, to try to grasp the way a non-westerner thinks. I was pleased to read recently that Mt. Holyoke had now included some knowledge of a non-western civilization in its requirements. When, in the early fifties, I suggested such a requirement for Douglass students to the educational policy committee, alas, even the other committee members were not interested to propose it to the full faculty. How helpful it might have been if members of our State Department had been aware of the revolutionary fervor in the Moslem religion which sparked the opposition against the Shah of Iran and held Americans hostage for over a year!

I hardly need add that the ability to speak and write the English language remains the mark of an educated American. It is important also that good students and certainly graduate students in the social studies and humanities be helped in the material they are writing upon to analyze, to synthesize, and to generalize.

Increasingly the ability to use a computer is becoming a necessity for all students (from grammar school through college). Its assistance in fostering quantitative thinking is at present often pointed out by educators. I do, however, deplore the fact that too often even a college graduate uses a computer to add .98 and .62. The reader may have noticed, on the other hand, that nothing has been said about a required survey course of western civilization, important as it is that an educated person knows and respects our heritage. I believe such a course must be most selective in the topics lectured upon, read, and discussed, and taught by the best or most experienced professors if it achieves its purpose. Such a course might well be most valuable if required of seniors, rather than of freshmen.

Do the faculty have a responsibility beyond their major jobs of teaching and research? In my opinion, the answer is yes. Would that more members of the faculty focused on education as a whole as well as on their own specific concerns and those of their own departments! Although teaching and research have been my main concern throughout the years, personally I have been glad I could play a part in the college and university as a whole. If occasionally the committee work seemed time-consuming and the tangible results slim or negligible, in retrospect I am more and more convinced of the importance of active participation in the college or university of which you are a part.

Such participation means also that you are willing and available to counsel your own students when they or you see the need. There are many times when a word from you will be of real value to them and, conversely, when a question from them a help to you. When one bright freshman, a contributor to class discussion, who received a flunking grade on her first test, was asked to come to my office and questioned as to the six, she began to work hard, and eventually majored in history, received high honors as a senior, and took graduate courses in history. George Schmidt wrote concerning my attitude:

You never felt it necessary to wrap yourself in an arena of pedantic aloofness or to affect the conceit of professorial unapproachability, but were at all times accessible to your students and sympathetic with their hopes and fears. And you kept yourself deeply involved in the workaday affairs of the college and university.[1]

It must be admitted, however, that, the larger the institution is, the lower the priority such participation seems to have in the factors considered when a professor is evaluated by his colleagues for promotion—and particularly for associate and full professorships. It is his published research that seems to matter, while his general contribution to the institution, and also the *quality* of his teaching, count too little in his promotion. Is it because such factors are unimportant or cannot quantitatively be weighed?

As one looks at higher education in 1984 and peers into the future, many doubts and questions arise. Here are a couple. To what extent and in

1. From the letter of George Schmidt, chairman of the Douglass department from 1932 to 1955, read at my "retirement" party in May 1966.

what ways can quality education continue—or will liberal arts education take on more and more the characteristics of mass production, too often with shoddy results? As it becomes more and more difficult for a liberal arts graduate to find a job, can curricula be devised better combining liberal arts courses with professional ones?[2]

Among the hopeful trends, as one peers into the future, is the fact that more and more older people are coming to college. One of my most brilliant students entered when she was in her late twenties, stayed out for a year to have her first child and another year for her second, but persisted and graduated with high honors in history, received a Woodrow Wilson Fellowship and a Princeton Ph.D., and is at present a professor at an eastern college.[3] One member of the seminar I taught at the Bunting Institute at Radcliffe in 1968/9 was the eighty-year-old Boston woman whom I have already mentioned: she wrote me a letter to say how

2. Such a curriculum has been devised and will be put into effect soon by the Polytechnic Institute of New York. See the *New York Times*, February 2, 1983. In the past year, more institutions have been working out such curricula.

3. In the *Times Literary Supplement* of March 30, 1984, Routledge & Kegan Paul announced the publication of a book by this former student: *"Family Life in the Seventeenth Century* by Miriam Slater. In this pioneering study of the Verney family, based on more than 10,000 family letters and papers, Professor Slater shows how a family of county gentry lived and behaved at a time of political and social crisis."

much this intellectual experience meant to her life, even though she realized that she wasn't "as quick or sharp" as the younger students in the seminar.

In their long history, universities, beginning in Bologna, Paris, and Oxford in Europe in the twelfth century and spreading to Cambridge and New Haven, Palo Alto and Berkeley in the new world, have never ignored the liberal education of their students. May this centuries-old belief in it live on as one of the West's major contributions to our present and future world!

Retirement Years: since 1967

BEFORE MY RETIREMENT at the end of June 1967
I had received offers to teach at New York
University and Northwestern University, but decided for various reasons not to accept them. (I
did, however, as previously mentioned, teach a graduate seminar at the Radcliffe Bunting Institute during the first semester of 1968/9.)

Consequently my retirement years were spent
right here where I had worked for thirty-nine years,
and in retrospect I believe that they were happy and
productive ones. My most important objective was
to complete the research begun in England in 1952
and 1955 and write two short books: *The Political
Thought of Sir Henry Vane the Younger*,[1] and
From Tradition to Political Reality.[2] In my opinion
the latter is the better, although neither can be
compared with *The Crisis of the Constitution*. During the seventies I did considerable research upon

1. University of Pennsylvania Press, 1969.
2. *Studies in British History and Culture*, Vol. VII, Archon
Books, 1980.

Charles I,[3] but gave up any thought of writing an essay upon him.

The resources of the Alexander Library at Rutgers made it possible to read many of the new books and articles on the Tudor-Stuart period. Having taught only European history, I now read some of the newer books in American history. I also continued to follow my longtime concern with international problems and policies. As the passing years have increasingly brought new health problems, resulting in diminishing physical and nervous strength, I am eternally grateful that my eyes remain among my better parts, allowing me to read a great deal.

After my retirement I cooperated with my successor, Professor Maurice Lee, in directing the Ph.D. dissertation of Cordelia Smith, for he said that I knew more than he about her subject. After she received her Ph.D. she has continued to consult both of us concerning the publication of parts of it.[4]

My interest in the Conference on British Studies has continued, and I have attended many of the sessions held in this area. In 1980, when a meeting was held at Rutgers dealing with new research on the background of the civil war, I acted as chairman.

3. See p. 53.
4. The Philosophical Society has accepted for publication an article taken from it.

At Commencement in 1967 (l. to r.: Katherine Drinker Bowen, Margaret Judson, Judge Brennan, Mrs.
White, President Gross)

At Lake Spofford

It is good to live in a university community, with its numerous opportunities to attend lectures and seminars, to enjoy wonderful music (both symphonic and chamber), and to follow the changing art displays in the Voorhees Art Museum. My colleagues in history, both at Douglass and at Rutgers College, have often invited me to their academic and social functions. To hear and come to know Christopher Hill when he was in residence in the first semester of 1981/2 was an experience I treasure. The executive director of the Douglass Alumnae Association, Adelaide Zazorin, and the recent Douglass deans, Margery Foster, Jewel Cobb, and above all Mary Hartman, have graciously included me at many of the Douglass functions.

It has been possible for me in retirement to become more involved than in my active years in community affairs. Since 1972 I have been on the board of directors of the Middlesex Family Service Association, a unit of the national association. Our work with families needing trained counsellors, with battered children turned over to us by the court, with the aging, etc., has revealed to me areas of society of which I had long been too ignorant. To function on a board made up of men and women from different walks of life, often with sharp disagreements as to our policies, was an education in itself.

Since its founding in 1955 I have been active in

the New Brunswick unit of the English Speaking Union. Several times I have served on its board of directors, but I always refused to be its president.[5] The talks I have given at monthly dinner meetings were on Queen Elizabeth I, on Henry VIII, and (in April 1983) on my research and life in England, where I went so many times to study between 1926 and 1973. In August 1968 I was fortunate to act as a delegate of the New Brunswick E.S.U. at the world conference held in Edinburgh. The president, Prince Philip, presided over many of the sessions. He and Queen Elizabeth were living at the time in Holyroodhouse, and the E.S.U. delegates attended their garden party on the grounds of their Scottish home in August. The Queen and Prince Philip attended a reception for us in the beautiful library of the University of Edinburgh. Here they greeted each of us individually. I think I both curtsied to and shook hands with the Queen.

Since 1972 or '73 I have served on the four-member executive committee of the Association of Retired Rutgers Professors. Our major objective has been to try to increase the pensions of our oldest retirees—an objective which, alas, the committee

---

5. Upon retirement, I made the decision not to accept any office in any organization where I would have major responsibilities and deadlines to meet. I tried, however, to help in as many ways as possible.

failed to achieve. We did, however, secure or improve medical insurance for some older retirees, and set up a sum to which they may apply for financial help when in dire need. At present the committee is suggesting ways and means by which retired faculty may continue to feel and act as an integral part of the university. Over the years our committee has worked hard, but it has experienced many frustrations in a diffuse and rapidly growing university whose administrators seem at times to give our concerns a low priority.

Although I have not participated to any extent in its numerous activities, Christ Church in New Brunswick, where I am a communicant, has been a source of strength for me. Its music, so integral a part of a worship service, achieves a high standard, too seldom found in a small city. I was pleased to be asked to give, at one of the coffee-hours after the church service, a talk on the history of the Anglican Church from the time of its separation from Rome under Henry VIII until its reestablishment, after Mary Tudor, under Elizabeth. A number in the audience seemed interested to hear this story given by a historian.

Last, but not least: it has been and continues to be most interesting and rewarding to participate in the activities of the Travellers Club of New Brunswick, an organization 102 years old, which I joined in

1972. Each year its program committee selects a theme for the year, and then chooses topics relevant to that theme upon which twice a month two short papers (theoretically of twenty minutes each) are read and discussed by the members. When women were the theme for two years, I wrote on Queen Elizabeth and on Queen Mary; on "The Impact of Science" when the eighteenth century was the theme; Lord Durham when we studied Canada; Sun Yat Sen when it was China; and when it was Russia, I wrote on Russia in World War One and the Russian revolutions in 1917. Paris in the twelfth century was another paper I gave, and in 1983 it was Saint Thomas More, when the theme was "Greatness in our Western Heritage."

The twenty-five to thirty members of this organization are interesting individuals, and I was delighted to come to know those whom I had never met before. At an age when too many longtime friends had died, it was a joy to find new friends among the Travellers.

Like many retirees, I traveled in the flesh as well: across Canada to British Columbia in 1968, to England again in 1968, '71, '73, and '77, to Ireland in 1968, and to Vienna, Greece and the islands in 1971. My last trip abroad was made in 1980 with a Mt. Holyoke group, with whom I spent five days in Paris, two in Rouen, and seven in Provence, which

I had long hoped to visit. The trip was entitled "the Medieval Spirit," and the group included the president of Mt. Holyoke, Elizabeth Kennan. A medieval scholar, she gave a number of brilliant lectures to a non-academic group, as well as participating in our different ventures. In Provence we spent a night in the guest house of a nunnery and attended a Sunday service in a monastery where the monks sang the mass in Gregorian chant. Our days in Avignon, home in the fourteenth century of the pope, and our trips from there to fascinating places such as Carcassonne and Arles, stand out in my memory, as do the meals where the local speciality, mussels in a delicious sauce or a pot-pourri, was served.

In addition to the organizations and group activities in which I have participated, I love a bridge game, a trip to nearby Princeton to shop, enjoy a meal, or visit an art gallery, or a ride in the country to see the dogwood growing wild in the New Jersey woods or the autumn colors in New Jersey, New Hampshire, or Vermont. On the deck of my Spofford Lake, New Hampshire, cottage many hours are quietly spent, often alone, watching the changing patterns of the lake's waters or the floating clouds in the sky.

Yes, I can truly say that my retirement years have been good ones.

Appendix

Awards and Honors

Phi Beta Kappa, Mt. Holyoke, 1921.
Graduate fellowships: Mt. Holyoke 2, Radcliffe 2.
Guggenheim Fellowship, 1954–55.
Alice Freeman Palmer Visiting Professor at the University of Michigan, 1959.
From Rutgers:

> Linbach award for distinguished teaching, 1962;
> University award for outstanding service, 1963;
> Honorary Doctor of Laws, 1968, at the 50th anniversary of Douglass.

Honorary Doctor of Letters, Mt. Holyoke, 1972, at my 50th reunion.
Fellow Royal Historical Society.
A Cup given me by the Conference on British Studies at the British Embassy in Washington, Dec. 1980, as one of the five living founders of the Conference in 1950.

Books Published

"Henry Parker and the Theory of Parliamentary Sovereignty, 1640–49" in *Essays in Honor of C. H. McIlwain*, Harvard University Press, 1936.

The Crisis of the Constitution, Rutgers University Press, 1949; rpt. Farrar, Straus & Giroux, 1964, 1971, 1976.

The Political Thought of Sir Henry Vane the Younger, University of Pennsylvania Press, 1969.

From Tradition to Political Reality, Archon Books, for the Conference on British Studies, 1980.

Subscribers

BUSINESS REPLY MAIL

FIRST-CLASS MAIL   PERMIT NO.8061   DES MOINES, IOWA

POSTAGE WILL BE PAID BY ADDRESSEE

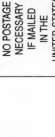

YANKEE®

PO BOX 37015
BOONE IA 50037-2015

Beautiful!

(The magazine and the price!)

☐ **YES!** Send me a year of *Yankee* and a FREE cookbook — *The Old Farmer's Almanac Favorite Cookies* — all for **only $24!** That's a **$6 savings** off the cover price!

Name _____

Address _____

City _____ State _____ Zip _____

Subscriptions outside US add $6 per year (US funds). Sorry, no billing available. (Canadian GST included in annual rate.)

Order on line at www.NewEngland.com/subcard

Send no money now! We'll bill you later!

D14MGAW

Professor Ruth M. Adams,
Dartmouth College
Professor Emily Alman,
Rutgers University
Professor John W. Baldwin,
Johns Hopkins University
Jenny M. Jochens
Matilda Cogan Barron
Professor Seymour Becker,
Rutgers University
Professor Elizabeth F. Boyd,
Rutgers University
Professor Robert G. Bradshaw,
Rutgers University
Jean R. Bradshaw
Prof. Harry C. Bredemeier,
Rutgers University
Agnes N. Brown
Professor Jean L. Burton,
Rutgers University
Professor Mildred Campbell,
Vassar College
Arthur H. Carpenter, Jr.,
in memory of
Dorothy C. Hiller
Jean A. Carpenter,
in memory of
Dorothy C. Hiller
Professor Fred A. Cazel, Jr.,
University of Connecticut
Professor Peter Charanis,
Rutgers University
Professor Evalyn A. Clark,
Vassar College
Phyllis Lynne Clarke
Professor Sandi E. Cooper,
University of Richmond
Professor David L. Cowen,
Rutgers University
Margaret M. Dahm

Professor Margaret G. Davies,
Pomona College
Carol Witte DeLong
Prof. Mildred Moulton Doak,
Rutgers University
Dean Mary Maples Dunn,
Bryn Mawr College
Elizabeth W. Durham
Elizabeth G. Durkee
Professor Elmer C. Easton,
Rutgers University
Dean Tilden G. Edelstein,
Rutgers University
Anne C. Edmonds
Elizabeth B. Ellis, in memory
of Professor L. Ethan Ellis,
Rutgers University
English Speaking Union,
New Brunswick
Helen S. Flemer
Prof. Elizabeth Reed Foster,
Bryn Mawr College
Dean Margery Somers Foster,
Former Dean,
Douglass College
Frank R. Garfield
Marjorie H. Garfield
Professor Lora D. Garrison,
Rutgers University
Doris D. Gelman
Prof. Max Gideonse,
Rutgers University
Isabel A. Gideonse
Professor John R. Gillis,
Rutgers University
Prof. Penina Migdal Glazer,
Hampshire College
Professor Gerald N. Grob,
Rutgers University
Dean Frances P. Healy,
Russell Sage College

Professor Dorothy O. Helly,
Hunter College

Professor J. H. Hexter,
Yale University and
Washington University

Professor Christopher Hill,
Oxford University

Bridget Hill

C. Harrison Hill, Jr.

Patricia M. Hill

Sara J. Holiner

Gladys Collins Hunter

Miriam T. Irwin

Laurel W. Joiner

Edith Erickson Peters Jones,
Academic Dean,
Claremont College,
University of Cincinnati

Dean Mary Frear Keeler,
Hood College

Mary L. Keim

President Elizabeth T. Kennan,
Mount Holyoke College

Dr. Elisabeth G. Kimball

Professor Eugene E. Kuzirian,
University of Texas
at El Paso

Professor Phyllis S. Lachs,
Rutgers University

Professor Ann J. Lane,
Colgate University

Louisa Hofstetter Lavelle

Professor Suzanne D. Lebsock,
Rutgers University

Professor Maurice Lee, Jr.,
Rutgers University

Anna West Lloyd

Phyllis Talluto Logie

Dawn Lospaluto

Professor Jessie G. Lutz,
Rutgers University

Margaret G. Lynch

Professor Bryce D. Lyon,
Brown University

Prof. Wallace T. MacCaffrey,
Harvard University

Prof. Richard L. McCormick,
Rutgers University

Prof. Richard P. McCormick,
Rutgers University

Prof. Katheryne McCormick,
Rutgers University

Professor J. Sears McGee,
University of California
at Santa Barbara

Professor Eric L. McKitrick,
Columbia University

Edyth S. McKitrick

Norma W. Melick

Mount Holyoke College
Library

Professor Edith D. Neimark,
Rutgers University

Dean Edna M. Newby,
Former Associate Dean,
Douglass College

Professor John P. Newton,
Rutgers University

Priscilla M. Newton

Professor Emiliana P. Noether,
University of Connecticut

Dr. Janet L. Norwood

Joyce Reinert Ochs

Professor Alison G. Olson,
University of Maryland

Professor John W. Osborne,
Rutgers University

Professor Cyrus R. Pangborn,
Rutgers University

Ann M. Peterson

Professor Sidney Ratner,
Rutgers University

Jean Lederer Rich

Dean Frances E. Riche,
Former Assistant Dean,
Douglass College
Professor Caroline Robbins,
Bryn Mawr College
Peg Saenz Roberts
Prof. Madeline R. Robinton,
Brooklyn College
Professor James N. Rosenau,
University of
Southern California
Mollie Schwartz Rosenhan
Professor Herbert H. Rowen,
Rutgers University
Marion Short Sauer
Elizabeth S. Sauter
Edith K. Schapiro
Janice Capaccio Scheer
Professor Richard Schlatter,
Rutgers University
Mildred Saks Schlesinger
Professor George P. Schmidt,
Douglass College,
Rutgers University
Irma G. Schmidt
Prof. Gordon J. Schochet,
Rutgers University
Professor Lois G. Schwoerer,
George Washington Univ.
Jean O'G. Sheehan
Sally Africa Skillings
Professor Miriam Slater,
Hampshire College
Dr. Alice Kimball Smith
Dr. Cornelia D. Smith
Eleanor Kahn Smith
Margaret F. Smith
President Mary Bunting
Smith, Former Dean,

Douglass College
Former President,
Radcliffe College
Professor John Spielman,
Haverford College
Danila Spielman
Prof. Peter D. L. Stansky,
Stanford University
Robert D. Stillman
Joan C. Stillman
Nancy E. Stillman
Professor Lawrence Stone,
Princeton University
The Stratford Historical
Society, Stratford, Conn.
Elaine G. Strauss
Helen H. Torrey
Dean Marjorie M. Trayes,
Former Dean of Students,
Douglass College
Professor Thomas Weber,
Douglass College,
Rutgers University
Barbara Sheppard Webster
Eleanor M. Webster
Barbara L. Weigel
Elizabeth Tilton Welsh
Provost Kenneth W. Wheeler,
Rutgers University
Dr. Philip H. Wheeler
Elizabeth P. Wheeler
Dr. Virginia P. Whitney
Frances Bickelhaupt Wilcox
Emma Burch Williams
President Henry R. Winkler,
University of Cincinnati
Carl R. Woodward, Jr.
Alice F. Woodward